Exploring the Visual Arts

Exploring
the Visual Arts

Burton Wasserman
Professor of Art
Glassboro State College
Glassboro, New Jersey

Davis Publications, Inc.
Worcester, Massachusetts

Printed in the United States of America
Library of Congress Catalog Card Number: 76-19938
ISBN: 0-87192-085-9

Printing: Davis Press, Inc.
Type: 10/13 Optima by Williams Graphic Service, Inc.
Design: Penny Darras, Thumbnail Associates

10 9 8 7 6 5 4 3 2 1

Cover illustration adapted from *Number Forty-three,*
silkscreen print by the author.

Contents

We often take our ability to see for granted. But just for a moment, think about what life would be like if a window shade was pulled down all around you and you couldn't see anything anymore. It's a bleak prospect, isn't it? There's so much you would miss. For example, trees, people, animals, surf, sky, and stone. Taken together, these items are a catalog of visual relationships rich with variations of line, shape, color, texture, pattern, and space.

Design in Nature

The accompanying photographs are representative of the beauty and diversity of form existing in the natural world. Hopefully, the time spent with these pictures will encourage further study on your own. Through personal observation, you will see countless details you might otherwise overlook.

Many of our most cherished ideas about beauty have come from looking directly at nature. From the shape of an egg to a tiny snowflake, we see examples of design that are basically functional and also attractive. Perhaps you have already experienced the fascination that comes from seeing the ever-changing light of the sun, the colors on the wings of a butterfly, or the shifting shapes of clouds floating through the sky.

There is so much to see in our immediate environment. But until we focus on something specific, it is all a vague blur. However, when we stop and carefully consider the shapes and colors in natural objects, we can see how they are constructed. With

Nature presents an endless catalog of design forms. Here, light reflected on the surface of the water shimmers with brightness beside the dark silhouettes of boats and people. (Photograph by Larry Conrad)

Chapter One

An Invitation to Personal Enrichment

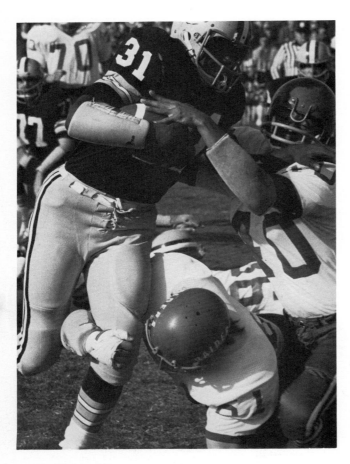

Figures in motion suggest a dynamic pattern of constantly changing shapes. (Photograph by David Conrad)

further study, we can also see how everything from a blade of grass to the distant stars fits together in the vast, all-encompassing order of nature.

The more you see and are sensitive to, the more you are bound to enrich yourself. By trying to enjoy nature, you will become familiar with an endless variety of design. Furthermore, you don't have to pay any admission fee to see the free show all around you.

Design in the Human Environment

Besides the riches of nature, there are many things to see that have been put together by human hands. Don't miss the fascinating forms you can find in such commonplace objects as slats in a fence or a big city skyline.

If you take time to look at things carefully, you will find all sorts of patterns everywhere. As you focus attention on buildings, you will frequently find them covered with brickwork patterns in different colors. In large structures especially you are apt to see a repeating pattern of windows. Houses, fence pickets, streetlights, and automobiles lined up in a row present additional examples of interesting patterns. Because you see these patterns so frequently, you may take them for granted. But if you take advantage of what there is to see, you can enjoy many fascinating experiences.

What is true of pattern is equally true of all other design elements. Think of the countless shapes, textures, and colors you can discover if you open your eyes and take in everything that surrounds you.

Stones lying on the ground reveal a surprising variety of shapes and textures. (Photograph by Larry Conrad)

The sea beside a rocky shoreline offers an endless display of agitated action. (Photograph by Peggy Diamond)

The urban scene is rich in all kinds of repeating patterns and contrasting shapes. Like giant fingers reaching upward, the tall buildings of San Francisco connect the sky above with the earth below. (Photograph courtesy of the Transamerica Corporation)

A balanced sense of order can be felt in this design made of gray shadows, bright highlights, and wooden fence slats. (Photograph by Burton Wasserman)

Design from the Hand of the Artist

By training ourselves to see with increased awareness, we also refine our ability to react keenly and critically to what other people have created in a language of visual expression. We may thus become more responsive to what artists have made throughout the years, yesterday as well as today. With a heightened sensitivity to form, we are more likely to enjoy their work.

Normally, everyone sees the world from within the limitations of his or her specific life. All our past personal experiences shape the way we perceive people and events at any given moment. However, by looking into the work of an artist, we can get a new perspective. We can go outside ourselves for a little while and see the world through someone else's eyes. Think of how much more you will feel and know, simply by spending time with the work of different artists.

No matter how silent a work of art may seem to be, it has an amazing capacity for talking to us, if we pay attention to what it has to say in the language of design. Beyond our most minimal physical needs, all of us seek experience with activities that give us an enriched sense of well-being. This explains why people since the beginning of time have reached out to enjoy visual forms whenever and wherever they could find them, in the arts as well as in nature and the human environment.

Design is Everywhere

Your eyes tell you more than just what they see. They also report how things feel. By the interplay of light, shadow, and structure, you know whether a surface will be smooth or rough, hairy, prickly, pleasant or unpleasant to your sense of touch.

Seeing such differences of texture has a lot to do with helping your senses feel wide awake and full of life.

The human eye is incredibly sensitive to differences of color and tone. Like texture, color is also capable of stimulating our senses to deep levels of emotional awareness. Think of all the different times you are affected by the colors you notice. Aren't you fascinated by the way colors seem to shift with changes in light and atmosphere? Aren't you intrigued by the variations of light and dark that seem to envelop everything?

Of course, simply recognizing visual elements such as textures, colors, and patterns is not all there is to see in a design. What makes visual experience significant is *how* these elements are organized in relation to each other.

Typically, the eye tends to favor harmony rather than discord. However, too much harmony can be monotonous. Consequently, we search for variety to keep our interest alive. Visual interest is also stimulated by rhythm within any arrangement of forms.

Along these same lines of reasoning, a well-organized design should be successfully balanced. Without equilibrium, there is an uncomfortable sensation of elements distributed carelessly and unevenly. Thus, they feel awkward and out of harmony with each other.

Finally, unless all the factors in a design are successfully integrated into one composite whole, whatever we examine is just an assortment of random parts. No matter how interesting they may be as separate pieces, they can never add up to a grand oneness if they are not unified in some way that holds them together visually. Typically, unity may be achieved by a line element that ties things together, by a repetition of a particular pattern, tex-

Human interest and visual forms have been combined in this painting to create a powerful design. Edward Hopper. *Nighthawks*. Oil on canvas. Collection of The Art Institute of Chicago. (Photograph courtesy of The Art Institute of Chicago)

By the magic touch of his brush, Rafael Rivera García transforms the blank wall of a housing project into a colorful mural. (Photograph courtesy of the Economic Development Administration, Commonwealth of Puerto Rico)

Two figures come alive in paint on canvas. Barkley Hendricks. *Ralph and Alvin*. Oil on canvas. (Photograph courtesy of the artist)

ture, or color, or by some other design device that serves to bind the various elements to each other.

Obviously, there is a lot more to look at in the world than meets the eye at first glance. Therefore, the more you consciously get involved with looking at things, the more you are going to see.

ACTIVITIES TO EXPLORE:

1. Find three repeating patterns in your home or school and three more out of doors. Sketch the patterns with crayon or make pictures of them with a camera.

2. Visit a zoo or a park and observe the forms of nature you find there.

3. Visit an art museum and take note of how painters and sculptors use color, pattern, and texture to enrich and dramatize what they have expressed in their work.

4. Make a collection of leaves and trace their outlines on paper with pencil. If your school has a photographic darkroom, make photograms with what you have gathered outside.

5. See what kinds of shapes you can identify in various plants, animals, and other forms of nature you can obtain for study.

6. Select an artist whose work interests you and stirs your feelings. What can you find out about this person by checking into books in the library? You might want to make your choice from among the following important figures from the past and the present.

Vincent van Gogh	Pablo Picasso
Mary Cassatt	Rembrandt
Leonardo da Vinci	Louise Nevelson
Piet Mondrian	Michelangelo
Alexander Calder	Salvador Dali

Professional designers aim to create products for daily use that are comfortable and attractive. (Photograph of bean-bag seating courtesy of the Futorian Corporation)

Though it was made more than a hundred years ago, this Shaker bench looks as modern as any furniture built to-day. Shaker Settee. Made at Enfield, New Hampshire; 1855. Owned by Mr. and Mrs. Julius Zieget and repro-duced with their permission. (Photograph courtesy of the Philadelphia Museum of Art)

Without the contributions made by many different product designers, contemporary life might be visually unappealing and extremely dull. Think of how colors and patterns in your clothes, home furnishings, and everything else you see and touch during a normal day have been created for your pleasure and personal use. How would you feel if they were all the same color and monotonous to look at in every other way?

The Importance of Well-designed Clothes

Among the many different areas of creative activity in the visual arts, few affect such great numbers of people as much as the field of clothing design. After all, nothing touches all of us more closely everyday than what we wear.

Generally speaking, clothes fulfill three important functions: protection, comfort and personal appearance.

Clothing designers use different colors and textures of fabric as an artist uses paint to make a picture. Finding distinctive qualities in a given piece of cloth, they then seek to express the fabric's mood and character in garments that are wearable and visually appealing. On occasion, it may seem as though some new fabric has been created for the sole purpose of becoming a special piece of clothing. On the other hand, many of the latest fashions are made from familiar fabrics that are handled in a creative manner.

At Home with Design

Another important area of design concerning everyone involves the appearance of the place where they live. To make personal decisions about

Chapter Two

Everyday Life—Made Better by Design

interior furnishings, people have to ask themselves what colors and materials they want in their homes.

The needs of all the different people who live together in a certain place should be taken into account when ideas for furnishing a home are explored. Personal patterns of work, rest, recreation, eating, and sleeping provide useful starting points for finding solutions suitable to a particular family's style of life. What fits one family well may be all wrong for another.

Planning and furnishing a home today is probably more exciting and challenging than it ever was in the past because of the wide range of materials and accessories that are currently available. Because of modern industry, we have great freedom of choice as we use furniture, fabrics, paint, and lighting to make living spaces filled with attractive shapes, colors, and textures.

Modern interiors may be severely formal or swingingly informal. A home can include romantic styles from the past alongside contemporary furnishings and be quite right for the people who live there. In short, interiors need not be limited to any single style. Unless one feels an urgent need for consistency of style, a *collected* look may prove to be more interesting and enjoyable.

As you are exercising individual choice in creating a home interior, several guidelines may be very sound and helpful. Simplicity and ease of maintenance can be important considerations. You may also want to ask yourself how durable and functional your selections will prove to be. For example, suppose a lounge chair looks very elegant but fails to support people comfortably when they sit in it. Obviously, a chair that can't do the basic job for which it was made is not worth getting unless you

just want to have it around as a piece of sculpture. On the other hand, a piece of furniture, no matter how substantial it may be, should also be attractive. There really is no good reason for a well-built object to look ungainly. The same can be said for every item of the total interior in which you choose to live.

Industrial designers seek to improve and beautify whatever people touch and use, from home furnishings to the kitchenwares used in preparing and serving meals. Generation Mist. Stoneware. Designed by Niels Refsgaard for Dansk International Designs Ltd. (Photograph courtesy of Dansk International Designs Ltd)

The earliest successful experimental telephone of 1876 looks primitive by comparison with what we have today. (Photograph courtesy of American Telephone and Telegraph Company)

The Work of the Industrial Designer

Besides clothes and home interiors, many other designed objects touch our daily lives at every turn. They include an endless variety of manufactured products.

Throughout the years, designers have fashioned useful articles for people. For example, when a knight needed protective armor, the armorer came forward with equipment appropriate to medieval combat. Likewise, the birchbark canoe of the early American Indians proved to be a sound solution to the basic need people had, back then, for safe, swift transportation across deep waterways. Of course, designing products today calls for solutions that are quite different from those worked out years ago. Modern technology and modern materials make possible a range of solutions that simply were not possible in the past.

The Industrial Revolution brought power machinery into almost every field of manufacturing. Today, the use of machines makes it possible to produce many useful products rather inexpensively and in quantities that would have once seemed impossible. Developing designs and forms for such mass production involves an understanding of consumer needs as well as manufacturing processes.

As the accompanying pictures illustrate, industrial designers constantly seek to improve and beautify everything people touch and use. An especially good example which shows the structural as well as stylistic changes made over the years in a specific product is the telephone. As you look at the photographs here, you can see how progress has been made in both the form and function of this remarkable instrument

Latest in the long line of telephone advances is the twelve-button Trimline instrument which combines handset and Touchtone push buttons in one lightweight unit. (Photograph courtesy of American Telephone and Telegraph Company)

Examples of the Eastern Air Lines logotype. (Photographs courtesy of Eastern Air Lines Incorporated)

Graphic Communications

Today, more than ever before, we are exposed to pictures and all sorts of other two-dimensional designs. Hardly a day goes by when we do not look at dozens of photographs, films, television images, and published materials of all kinds. While some of these designs are not especially attractive, many others are quite handsome in appearance and imaginative in approach. In either case, none of them would exist if it were not for the creative people who designed them in the first place.

Perhaps more so than any other type of creative artwork, graphic visuals are the true expression of the modern era, an age of exploding information and instant communication. After only a few seconds or, at most, a month of exposure, the television title and magazine illustration are often forgotten. In spite of this short life, however, the fast-growing field of graphic design includes many of the brightest and most inventive talents in art.

Clearly, good design in the field of graphic communication calls for the projection of strong ideas capable of making their point quickly and clearly. In order to attract a spectator's eye and command continued attention, all unnecessary details have to be eliminated. What remains must be visually interesting and appealing. For example, the design of a trademark or poster has to be appropriate to the product it represents, conveying the qualities of that product with distinction and brevity. The viewer should be able to quickly identify the product when seeing the design. Forms that are cluttered, complicated, or confusing would fail to carry out their purpose. For this reason, many successful businesses have come to recognize and appreciate the value a well-designed, up-to-date visual symbol

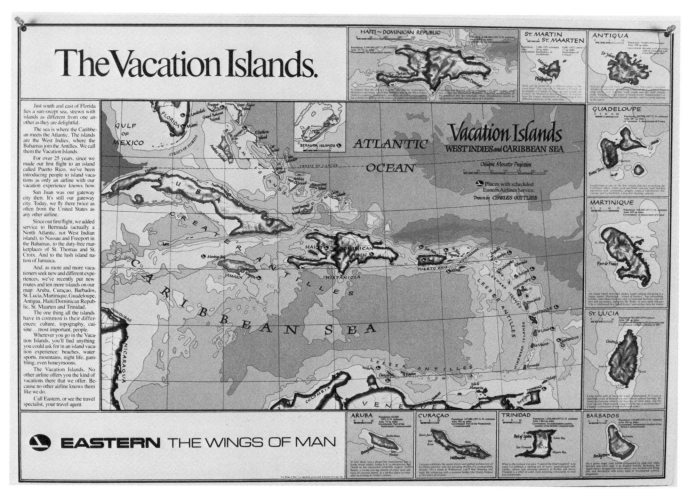

Example of the Eastern Air Lines logotype used in a poster
advertising travel to vacation islands in the Caribbean Sea.
(Photograph courtesy of Eastern Air Lines Incorporated)

Hardly anyone in America today would fail to recognize this visual symbol. Looking back at people from their TV sets, the familiar eye of CBS is like an old friend to millions of spectators across the country. Visual logotype for a television network. (Photograph courtesy of Columbia Broadcasting System, Inc.)

Logotype of the Philadelphia 76ers basketball team. (Photograph courtesy of Philadelphia 76ers Basketball)

or logotype, as well as other forms of graphic communication.

The field of graphic art seen by more people more often than any other field is design for television. The importance and impact of TV graphic art can be appreciated when you realize that the average child spends more time watching and listening to television than he spends with his teachers or parents. Furthermore, average adults may pass ten to fifteen years of their life span tuned in to television. Graphic designers for TV use lettering, type, photography, animation, live action, painting, collage, and sometimes even three-dimensional constructions. With these forms, the TV graphic designer has worked out a spare, imaginative style that has tremendously affected our ability to read and understand at a glance visual images and information. These effects spread to virtually every other area of art and communication.

Designers Enrich Your Life

Think of the many design decisions you constantly make. For example, as you start the day, you may ask yourself what you should wear, taking into account how your clothes will look when you put them on. From time to time you must decide between buying one article or another. Obviously, making such choices involves the way you feel about what you see. To help you, professional designers are constantly at work creating all sorts of products intended to offer enrichment and satisfaction. By studying what they provide, you are bound to become better informed about design. Naturally, the more you are informed, the better your personal decisions are going to be. Perhaps that single fact explains why caring about design can be so useful to you in everyday life.

More people watched the Super Bowl than any single event in the history of sports.

And most of them saw it on

SPORTS

CBS TELEVISION NETWORK

The CBS Television Network.

CTN audience estimates based on National Arbitron Ratings subject to qualification available on request.

Next season CBS will provide <u>exclusive</u> coverage of the Super Bowl, as well as all NFL games throughout the regular season.

Because it has such high recognition value, the CBS Television logotype is often used for advertising and promotional purposes. (Photograph courtesy of Columbia Broadcasting System, Inc.)

ACTIVITIES TO EXPLORE:

1. Make believe you are a judge for a competition of the best designs in the latest clothing styles being offered on the market. Put together a little scrapbook of your choice of the ten most attractive articles of wearing apparel you can find. Use newspapers and magazines you have at home or can get from friends and neighbors.

2. Visit a furniture store in your community and see what appeals to you. Take note of the colors and shapes in the various pieces you like. When you find selections you don't care for, ask yourself *why* they "turn you off."

3. Rummage around your house for odds and ends of different materials such as cloth, wood, plastic, and so on. Examine the textures and patterns you can distinguish in these various items you collected. Ask yourself which textures and patterns feel good and which ones do not. Can you explain why?

4. Make a collection of trademarks (logotypes) you like from different kinds of products that you find advertised in magazines and newspapers. Can you tell another person why you chose the ones you did?

5. Look around in the kitchen of your home and select three or four objects that take your fancy because of their shapes and colors. One at a time, turn them slowly in your hands to become more aware of their forms. Pick out two or three that you like best and sketch them. Try to arrange them into an interesting composite on your paper.

6. Can you find evidence of imaginative thought in various examples of industrial product design? Identify certain products which have been improved in either their appearance or function when compared with older versions of the same articles.

This poster by Sam Maitin is a powerful example of graphic design using simplified shapes and contrasting colors. (Photograph courtesy of the artist)

17/76 Achievement Fund

challenge goal $17,000,000

Equality through Education

United Church of Christ
support of
six AMA Colleges
and overseas educational projects

Sam Martin

Like clothing and food, shelter is one of the basic necessities of life. In our society, the people who design and supervise the construction of such settings are called architects. They create the buildings in which people carry on all their activities, safely protected from the weather. Typically, architects are responsible for conceiving well-planned homes, schools, hospitals, houses of worship, factories, and stores.

Chapter Three

Environments for Human Needs

The Architect Serves Society

Architects are imaginative as well as practical because they are artists as well as builders. On one occasion they may be asked to design a private house or an office building. On other occasions they may be called on to create groups of buildings and their surroundings or, in some instances, entire communities. In cooperation with engineers and urban planners, they design shopping areas, home developments, and civic centers. On very complex projects, an architect may be a member of a team which will also include landscape designers, sociologists, psychologists, interior designers, real estate experts, attorneys, economists, and others.

When an environmental planner is successful in designing an area, foot traffic is separated from vehicular traffic, people do not feel overwhelmed by their surroundings, and children are safe at play. In every other possible way, the affairs and concerns of people are brought into harmony with the

Architects and community planners develop environments designed with people in mind. A shopping center and surrounding recreation areas in Columbia, Maryland are shown here. (Photograph by the James Ferry Photograph Studio, courtesy of the Rouse Company, Columbia, Maryland.

The park and lakefront areas in downtown Chicago complement the nearby skyscrapers because they keep a sense of the human scale. (Photograph by Murphy Photography, courtesy of the city of Chicago, Department of Development and Planning)

3 New housing located on open landscaped plazas is an important element in the Golden Gateway redevelopment project of San Francisco, a site formerly filled with urban blight. (Photo by Dickey and Harleen Studios, courtesy of the San Francisco [California] Redevelopment Agency)

2 The KYW Building of Philadelphia is a fine example of a new building successfully integrated with the historic character of existing buildings and the landscape of the adjoining Independence Mall area. KYW Building. Broadcasting facilities and administrative offices; designed by Ballinger Architects and Engineers. (Photograph by Harris Davis, courtesy of KYW Radio and TV; Ballinger Architects and Engineers of Philadelphia, Pennsylvania.)

world of nature—clean and unspoiled. In a well-planned community, people can breathe fresh air and see greenery close at hand. Commercial and industrial development takes place only in certain zones removed from residential areas. Thus, people can enjoy peaceful relaxation and privacy in their homes.

Like individual human beings, communities also grow and change as they get older. In some instances, they improve with age. In other instances, if civic neglect and either poor planning or no planning at all have caused deterioration to set in, there is clearly a great need for renewal.

At its best, community restoration is a continuing process because good development grows out of a desire to enhance the present and plan for the future. For example, slum clearance and the provision of attractive housing for a city's residents are essential elements in modern designs for urban renewal. Likewise, when industrial and commercial plants become obsolete, they have to be updated in order to effectively serve the needs of people.

Another important aspect of positive community growth is the preservation of old structures that are still basically sound. In some instances, these structures may also have historic significance. They lend the present day a sense of richness that can only come from the passage of time and the gradual development of pride based upon a community's unique identity and heritage.

Because publicly supported renewal programs often operate on very limited budgets, they may fail to achieve any measure of aesthetic distinction. To avoid a sterile appearance, renewal architecture should have landscaping, sculpture, fountains, murals or other artwork integrated with the basic building forms. To insure this practice, some cities and states (such as Baltimore, Philadelphia, Hawaii, and Washington) have enacted legislation requiring that a small percentage of the total cost of a public construction project be used for art. Clearly, such thinking provides a worthwhile model other cities and states might do well to follow.

In some places, local artists, often working together with groups of young people, have undertaken the task of enriching their surroundings by painting murals on the exterior walls of large buildings. Inevitably, such public art changes the face of a neighborhood. Examples of this trend can be found all over the country.

Looking after the environment and its appearance cannot be left to professional planners alone. Maintaining a community or recreating one that has fallen into disrepair calls for a joint effort by all citizens as well as their elected officials. Only when everyone cooperates can ugliness and ruin be avoided, or if things have gone too far, made once more into an attractive environment where people may live and work harmoniously and productively.

How the Architect Works

When architects are employed to create a design, they research the project and make rough sketches of different ways in which the requirements of the job may be met. The chosen sketches are refined further in the form of ground-plan drawings, cross-section studies, and elevation views. Each elevation view shows one side of a potential structure seen from the outside. Perspective drawings are also made to show in a pictorial way how a building will look after construction is completed. Sometimes, three-dimensional models are made to give an even better idea of the projected design.

After the planned proposals are approved, detailed drawings are made of every single part of the building, and blueprints are prepared for the guidance of the construction contractor.

Early in the planning stages, such factors as a sense of order, harmony, balance, scale, rhythm, proportion, and unity are carefully taken into account. The function of the building and how well that function will be fulfilled are also very important ingredients in any successful architectural design. Likewise, the suitability of the materials selected for construction, the method of building, and the relationship of the building to its site must be resolved by a designer if all the environmental, aesthetic, and practical usage demands are to be met successfully.

Perhaps the most important single feature architects try to include in their plans is the one most difficult to explain in words. Beyond sheer visual appeal, practical value, and economic factors, designers aim to invest their work with an intangible spiritual quality. This mysterious and elusive inspiration can only come from the innermost resources and creative drive of the architect, just as it does for artists in other fields. No matter how mystical it may seem, when that quality is present, it has an extraordinary capacity for enhancing the lives of the people who will occupy a structure, regardless of the specific activities they may carry on there.

4 Water tumbles from a sculptured fountain made of 101 concrete boxes, located on the Justin Herman Plaza in the Golden Gateway redevelopment area of San Francisco. Design of the fountain by Armand Vaillancourt. (Photograph by Joshua Freiwald, courtesy of the San Francisco [California] Redevelopment Agency)

5 A view of the old congested marketplace area of San Francisco before the Golden Gateway renewal project was begun by the city's redevelopment agency. (Photograph courtesy of the San Francisco [California] Redevelopment Agency)

ONE BEDROOM–DEN/STUDY

A good idea of how a building or a group of buildings will look on the outside from a short distance away is presented in the perspective drawings that are prepared for a client by the architect. Perspective sketch of the Irongate Garden Apartments. (Drawing courtesy of the architect, Lester Philip Glass)

Floor plans show how the different interior areas of a building are located in relation to each other. Their size and function are also indicated. Floor plans from the Irongate Garden Apartments. (Drawings courtesy of the architect, Lester Philip Glass.)

The Modern Approach

Today, we live in an age when modern industrial technology has made available materials and building techniques that were unknown earlier. In addition, we live in a time when the march of science has had an enormous influence upon our ideas of comfort and convenience, upon our notions of time and space, and upon the relationships of people to each other. For this reason, architects today examine a given problem with a very analytical approach. They try to build forms that will meet today's needs with today's materials and today's technology. However, that does not mean the architect is only a scientist or an engineer. The modern architect aims to be a psychologist and an artist as well. As psychologists, architects must have a sensitive understanding and deep insight into human needs and wishes. They must be able to create forms that are emotionally gratifying to clients as well as satisfying to their needs for physical well-being. Finally, as artists, architects must inevitably come to terms with the language of three-dimensional design. Everything they build has the potential for expressing feelings and ideas in the unique way that is possible only in the world of the visual arts. In all these respects, the modern architect shares the hopes that have motivated great designers in every era of history.

6 Today, new homes for moderate-income families in Columbus Mall have replaced the old shambles that once stood there. The buildings and grounds are owned by a cooperative corporation made up of the people who live in the development. (Photograph by Cunningham-Werdnigg, courtesy of the New Haven Redevelopment Agency)

7 Before the Columbus Mall redevelopment program was implemented in New Haven, Connecticut, people lived in run-down housing in shabby surroundings. (Photograph courtesy of the New Haven Redevelopment Agency)

ACTIVITIES TO EXPLORE:

1. Write a list of changes you would make if it was in your power to improve the overall plan of your community. Don't overlook traffic patterns and the location of schools, stores, and hospitals for the maximum benefit of local residents.

2. Develop a sketch in full color for a mural you would like to see painted on the side of a large public building in your neighborhood. Take into account what you believe the mural should express and check to see if your design would carry out this purpose.

3. Assume you could locate greenery anywhere you wanted in the areas where you live and go to school. What would you like to see planted? Where? Why?

4. Try to arrange a visit to an architect's office to see the work done there. Prepare a list of questions to take with you which would help you learn more than you know now about the practice of architecture.

5. Make rough sketches for "the house of your dreams" in which you could have anything you wanted, regardless of the cost.

6. As a result of walking around in your community and carefully observing the architecture you find there, draw up a list of the major building materials you found. Do you think architects have to know about the different materials available for construction work? Why?

The elevation views here show the relationship of a building to its site. Elevation views of the Immig Residence, Colorado. (Drawing courtesy of the architect, Lester Philip Glass.)

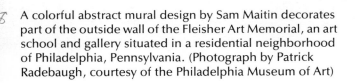

A colorful abstract mural design by Sam Maitin decorates part of the outside wall of the Fleisher Art Memorial, an art school and gallery situated in a residential neighborhood of Philadelphia, Pennsylvania. (Photograph by Patrick Radebaugh, courtesy of the Philadelphia Museum of Art)

9 Heroic efforts must have been needed in the initial arrangement of the massive stones. Today, no matter how dilapidated they are, the blocks still generate an awesome and mysterious presence. Stonehenge. Wiltshire, England. About 1800–1500 B.C. (Photograph courtesy of the British Tourist Authority, 680 Fifth Avenue, New York, New York)

10 The Sphinx gives an impressive image of the authority of the ancient pharaohs. The pyramids had a dual function: to protect the mummified king and to symbolize his absolute and godlike power. Great Sphinx and Pyramids. Giza, Egypt. About 2530 B.C. (Photograph courtesy of Egyptian Government Tourist Office, New York, New York)

Modern architects share in a heritage that goes back thousands of years. Many of the ideas and systems of construction in use today had their origins in the distant past. By taking some time to look back on yesterday, we can learn valuable lessons for dealing more effectively with our needs today.

The Ancient World

In prehistoric times, people sought shelter in caves and trees. By and by, they came to feel that raw natural enclosures were grossly inadequate. With these thoughts came the beginning of building construction.

Ancient Egypt produced temples and tombs that are still standing. Over forty-five hundred years ago, the Egyptians used post and lintel construction to erect huge pyramids and temples where priests could conduct the religious ceremonies which were important in their culture. In addition, they decorated what they built by carving and painting forms that illustrated their beliefs about life, death, and the hereafter.

Pure post and lintel construction was also used for Stonehenge, a grouping of monumental rock forms on the Salisbury Plain in southeastern England. Post and lintel construction, which continues to be used today, is a system in which the basic building unit consists of two or more upright posts supporting a horizontal beam.

The people of India, China, and Japan developed architectural styles that differed greatly from those of the West. Major structures were built to fulfill secular and religious needs. For example, the Taj Mahal at Agra in India provides a superb example of Eastern Islamic architecture because of its symmetry

Chapter Four

The Ancestors of Contemporary Architectural Form

and clarity of form. The Chinese built wooden temples and palaces from about 1000 B.C. to 200 B.C. Each of their towerlike buildings (called pagodas) had a spacious court leading to a high-roofed hall with graceful upwardly curving ledges. The Japanese also used wood as a construction material, but, on the whole, their style was lighter and more delicate than that of the Chinese.

Ancient civilizations were not confined to northern Europe, the Near East, and the Orient. Thousands of years before the current era, a lively society flourished in Mexico. Today, visitors can see examples of structures erected in various parts of the country long before the arrival of European explorers.

The flat-topped Pyramid of the Sun is seven hundred feet square at the base and as high as a twenty-story building. Unlike the pyramids of Egypt, this pyramid had outside staircases and a temple at the top. Pyramids at Teotihaucan, Mexico. Pyramid of the Sun is at the left, above. Built between A.D. 300 and 700. (Photograph courtesy of the Mexican National Tourist Council)

A stately white marble mausoleum, the Taj Mahal was built by the Shah Jehan as a memorial tribute to his favorite wife. Gardens and pools reflect the reserved elegance of the building. Taj Mahal. Agra, India. 1630–1652. (Photograph courtesy of the Information Service of India, Embassy of India, Washington, D.C.)

13 Considerable refinement is frequently evident in the details of Japanese architecture. Unusually responsive to nature, the Japanese also aim to coordinate a building with the surrounding rocks, trees, and shrubs located on the site. Japanese Tea House and Garden. Installed in the Philadelphia Museum of Art. 1910. (Photograph by A. J. Wyatt, Staff Photographer, courtesy of the Philadelphia Museum of Art)

14 For centuries the Parthenon has been a model of classic
order, balance, and dignity in architectural design. The
Parthenon. Designed by Ictinos and Calicrates. Athens,
Greece. 448–432 B.C. (Photograph courtesy of the Greek
National Tourist Office)

Some of the most important civilizations to emerge in the Western world were located on Crete in the Mediterranean Sea, on the islands of the Aegean Sea, and eventually on the mainland of Europe in the region now called Greece. Today, little is left of those early cultures. However, in their time, the ancient Greeks created architecture so magnificent that even now such temple ruins as the Parthenon on the Acropolis in Athens continue to command our attention because of their dignity, balance, and superb sense of order. Besides temples, the ancient Greeks also built open-air theaters. They were remarkably simple and admirably suited to their surroundings. Generally, the theaters were built into a hillside which provided a natural setting for the placement of great numbers of seats.

Equally important as the Greeks were the builders of ancient Rome. In addition to building aqueducts, bridges, roadways, and fortifications with great skill, Roman engineers contributed many new ideas to the field of architecture. For example, the Romans erected basilicas, oblong-shaped buildings with great interior spaces, which were used as bathhouses, law courts, and civic administrative offices. Of course, they also built temples in honor of their gods as well as houses, palaces, sports arenas, tall monuments, and triumphal arches.

16 Light for the building's interior comes in mainly through the open oculus (eye) in the center of the hemispheric dome. Because the building is circular, there are no corners anywhere. The interior of the Pantheon. Painting by Giovanni Paolo Panini from about 1750. National Gallery of Art, Washington, D.C., Kress Collection. (Photograph courtesy of the National Gallery of Art)

15 The interior grandeur of the Pantheon is but dimly suggested by the exterior view. The columns and triangular pediment are little more than a front porch for the after-structure: a huge dome-shaped roof supported by a drum made of massive masonry walls. The Pantheon. Rome, Italy. A.D. 118–125. (Photograph by S. D. Anderson, courtesy of Alinari)

Along with post and lintel techniques, the Romans made considerable use of the arch and dome. They used the principle of the arch to cover large rooms and halls with half-round ceilings called barrel vaults. Another device they put to work for spanning space in their buildings was the groin vault, made by intersecting two equal-sized barrel vaults over a square area. One more important practice of the Roman engineer-architects was their use of cement, concrete, and mortar as well as wood, glass, and metal in their buildings. Their skillfulness as builders is demonstrated by the fact that many of their structures, erected two thousand years ago, are still standing.

17 Ancestor of the modern football stadium, the Colosseum could accommodate more than fifty thousand spectators. The Colosseum. Rome, Italy. A.D. 72–80. (Photograph by S. D. Anderson, courtesy of Alinari)

18 In addition to using semicircular arch forms for spanning interior spaces, the ancient Romans also used these arches for monuments. The Arch of Constantine. Rome, Italy. A.D. 312–315. (Photograph by S. D. Anderson, courtesy of Alinari)

The Dark Ages and the Romanesque Period

The fall of the Roman Empire, about fifteen hundred years ago, began a period of history generally called the Dark Ages. During that time, great numbers of people lost their lives to barbarian invaders and to frightful diseases that sometimes wiped out entire populations. While humanistic culture suffered a decline, after flourishing vigorously during the preceding civilizations, the arts did not fade out altogether. Architecture in particular maintained continuous growth, especially in the area of church construction.

Early Christian architecture adopted two traditional Roman forms: the basilica and the round temple. The Roman approaches to spanning interior spaces were perfectly suited to the construction of large churches needed as the early Christian sects grew in size and influence. Typical examples from that period, still standing today in Italy, are the churches of San Appolinare near Ravenna and Santa Costanza in Rome.

The Byzantine style, a more cultivated version of the early Christian approach, flourished in the eastern portion of what had originally been the Roman Empire. The seat of Byzantine authority was located in Constantinople, today the city of Istanbul in Turkey. One of the greatest examples of Byzantine architecture that has successfully endured the passage of time and continues to attract the interest of visitors and students of art history is the Hagia Sophia in Istanbul.

By the year 800, the Western world began to show signs of recovery from the bleak period of invasions and decline. With the emergence of Christianity as a great unifying power in Europe,

19 The fundamental principle of traditional Byzantine architectural design, to achieve order by balancing masses and spaces against each other as perfectly as possible, found its highest expression in the mighty Hagia Sophia or Church of the Holy Wisdom. Today the building is a museum. Hagia Sophia. Designed by Anthemius of Tralles and Isidorus of Miletus. Istanbul, Turkey. A.D. 532–537. (Photograph, courtesy of the Information Counselor, Embassy of Turkey, Washington, D.C.)

The interior of this early Christian-period church is alive with shimmering light and color provided by rich marble surfaces and brilliant mosaic decorations. Basilica of San Apollinare. In Classe, near Ravenna, Italy. A.D. 533–549. (Photograph by S. D. Anderson, courtesy of Alinari)

many churches and church-related buildings were built. In response to the need for these new structures, there evolved a new architectural form called the Romanesque style. The basic characteristics of the new form were increased building size (compared with what had been built earlier), thick stone walls with small windows, round arches, and columns to support an overhead roof.

The Gothic Period

With the continued growth and influence of Christianity, Romanesque forms underwent a transformation which, in time, came to be called the Gothic style. Making use of creative engineering, the new style permitted the construction of higher and wider interior spaces. One of the main keys to the Gothic style was the use of pointed rather than round arches, which made increased height and width possible without an accompanying collapse of either the roof or the walls. For further assistance in dealing with the load problem, the builders introduced stone bridges called flying buttresses. These buttresses connected heavy reinforcing piers outside the walls with those places along the walls that were the main support of the mighty church roofs.

With vast wall areas relieved of the load-bearing burden, it became possible to put openings in the walls and then fill the openings with great stained glass windows. Besides permitting light to come in from outside, the windows also illustrated stories from the Bible as well as the lives of the saints and the Savior.

The exterior of Notre Dame de Paris includes many carved decorations, a grand triple doorway, and a huge rose window filled with stained glass. Notre Dame de Paris (west facade). Paris, France. 1163–1250. (Photograph courtesy of the Services Culturels de l'Ambassade de France, New York, New York)

Many people could be comfortably accommodated inside the great Gothic cathedrals. Notre Dame de Paris. Paris, France. 1163–1250. Interior view of the church pictured in a gouache painting by Viollet-le-Duc. (Photograph courtesy of the Services Culturels de l' Ambassade de France, New York, New York)

Though the Romanesque style was a distinct development with characteristics of its own, it made use of such typical Roman-period features as the round arch and cylindrical columns. Romanesque Cloister from the Abbey of Saint Genis des Fontaines. Twelfth century Installed in the Philadelphia Museum of Art. (Photograph by A. J. Wyatt, Staff Photographer, courtesy of the Philadelphia Museum of Art)

24 The photograph shows the graceful stone reinforcements called flying buttresses used to brace the main walls of Gothic cathedrals. The picture also illustrates gargoyles, the decorative sculptures that carried rainwater away from the roof. Notre Dame de Paris (exterior detail, viewed from the south approach). Paris, France. 1163–1250. (Photograph courtesy of the Service Culturels de l'Ambassade de France, New York, New York)

Another detail frequently seen on Gothic churches from the Middle Ages is called a gargoyle. It is actually a rainspout, carved in stone, usually in the shape of a demon, which channels water away from the roof in order to prevent interior leaks. Presumably, such an image was meant to ward off evil spirits who might want to play malicious pranks on those who came to offer devotions within the church. The appearance of the gargoyles and other carved details lends considerable richness to the overall profile of Gothic architecture.

The Renaissance Period

The Gothic period began to decline by the end of the fourteenth century. Gradually, it was replaced by a new development called the Renaissance. Specifically, Renaissance means a period of rebirth. In this case, the word refers to a revival of humanistic concerns similar to those widespread during the time of ancient Greece and Rome.

The Renaissance style was begun by Filippo Brunelleschi, a sculptor who was deeply interested in the art of ancient times. His engineering skill and aesthetic imagination enabled him to design a great dome to cover the Cathedral of Florence in 1420. His dome and his use of other details borrowed from the architectural forms of ancient Greece and Rome began to be widely copied. In almost no time at all, the new style was used in the construction of palaces and churches built during the fifteenth and sixteenth centuries. In England, the Renaissance style came to be called the Georgian style, arriving as it did during the period of the Georgian kings in the seventeenth and eighteenth centuries.

Classical Greek and Roman forms reappeared as ornamental devices in the architecture of the Renaissance. In this example, round and rectilinear elements have been rhythmically treated in a delicately balanced relationship. Pazzi Chapel. Designed by Filippo Brunelleschi. Florence, Italy. 1430–1433. (Photograph by S. D. Anderson, courtesy of Alinari)

The Baroque and Rococo Periods

Later developments of the Renaissance style came to be called the Baroque and the Rococo. In a very general sense, the Baroque is associated with the seventeenth century and the Rococo with the eighteenth century.

The Baroque at its height was an active exuberant style, compared with the quiet composure and sensitive restraint found in Renaissance forms. Filled with the theatrical, Baroque architecture tends to be awesome, impressive, and enormous.

One of the greatest examples of the Baroque style is the Basilica of Saint Peter's in Rome. This enormous church took many years to build and is topped by a huge dome designed by the famous artist Michelangelo.

Another dramatic example of the Baroque style is the Palace at Versailles built for King Louis XIV of France. The palace is a huge and rambling structure with seemingly endless miles of gardens stretching out in all directions from the main body of the building. The exterior walls of the palace seem to twist and turn with an inner sense of motion that is absolutely breathtaking.

With the death of Louis XIV in 1715, and the assumption of the French throne by Louis XV, architectual style underwent a decisive change. The grandeur of the classical Baroque was replaced by the dainty touch of the Rococo style.

The difference in the two styles is very evident as you step into rooms at the Palace of Versailles that were completed after the death of Louis XIV. Instead of deep reds, intense blues, and gold, there is a lavish use of pale tones of pink, baby blue, and eggshell white. The total effect is underscored by highly ornamental flowerlike and shell-like shapes, located almost everywhere, which are extremely ornate in a very playful yet fragile sort of way.

26 The Louvre (originally a royal palace) and its surrounding gardens communicate a sense of the awesome power exercised by the king of France during the Baroque era. Louvre Museum. Paris, France begun 1564. (Photograph courtesy of French Cultural Services, 972 Fifth Avenue, New York, New York)

27 For sheer splendor and Baroque magnificence, few buildings can equal the overwhelming interior of Saint Peter's Basilica in Rome. Giovanni Paolo Panini. The Interior of Basilica of Saint Peter, Rome. 1746. National Gallery of Art, Washington, D.C., Ailsa Mellon Bruce Fund. (Photograph courtesy of the National Gallery of Art)

24 The use of classic Roman details in the design of Jefferson's home was intended as an expression of his deep regard for the democratic virtues of the ancient Roman law. Monticello. Designed by Thomas Jefferson. Charlottesville, Virginia. 1770–1808. (Photograph courtesy of the Thomas Jefferson Memorial Foundation, Charlottesville, Virginia)

The Classical Revival, Victorian Gothic, and Eclecticism

Perhaps by way of reaction against the excessiveness of the Baroque and the daintiness of the Rococo, the early nineteenth century called for a return to older styles as sources of inspiration when new structures were built. First, there was a neoclassical development, sometimes called the Classical Revival. It was an effort at returning to the basic simplicity of classic Greek and Roman forms. Monticello, near Charlottesville, Virginia, designed by Thomas Jefferson for his personal use, is a good example of the Classical Revival at its best.

Next came Victorian Gothic, generally believed to have gotten underway because of the popularity of a book called *The Stones of Venice* by the British art critic John Ruskin. Victorian Gothic took the mannerisms of the Gothic style, such as the pointed arch and stone walls, but usually failed to include the monumental and awesome power of true Gothic forms as they appear in the great cathedrals from the medieval era. Sometimes, Victorian Gothic is called Scholastic Gothic because the style was widely used in college and university buildings.

With a further passage of time, architects took to mixing together various features from different periods of the past into a single new building. Such practice is called Eclecticism. Theoretically, the process was supposed to produce something better than any one style could ever produce by itself. However, all to often, Eclecticism resulted in a hodgepodge appearance.

In contrast to Eclecticism, certain developments were beginning to take shape during the latter half of the nineteenth century which prepared the foundation for the evolution of modern architecture.

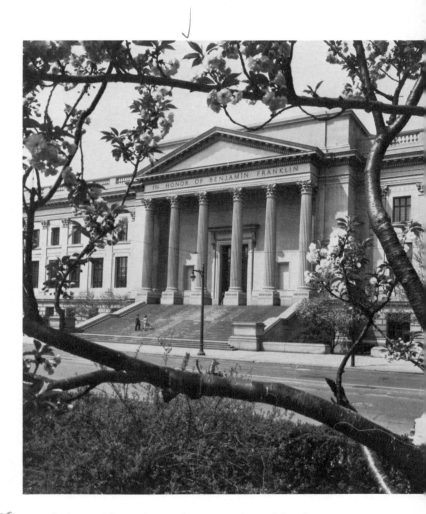

29 Details from old Greek temples were adopted for the facade (front side) of the Franklin Institute, a museum of science and industry. Franklin Institute. Philadelphia, Pennsylvania. 1934. (Photograph courtesy of The Philadelphia Convention and Tourist Bureau)

31 The use of steel for the structural framework of a building (such as this example) soon led to the widespread practice of erecting skyscrapers and to the emergence of a new approach to design in the field of architecture. Carson, Pirie, Scott Building. Designed by Louis Sullivan. Chicago, Illinois. 1899–1904. (Photograph courtesy of the Carson, Pirie, Scott and Company)

30 The Eiffel Tower showed how industrial materials and construction techniques could create a fresh building style appropriate to the modern era. Eiffel Tower. Designed by Gustave Eiffel. Paris, France. 1887. (Photograph courtesy of the French Cultural Services, 972 Fifth Avenue, New York, New York)

The Doorway to the Modern Era

With the arrival of the Industrial Revolution and the increasing availability of iron, architects began replacing stone with iron as the supporting structure of a building. An especially daring design was conceived and built by Sir Joseph Paxton in 1851. It was the Crystal Palace, made of a metal framework filled with clear glass panes, erected to house the London World's Fair of 1851.

The Crystal Palace was one of the first great prefabricated buildings of the world. The elements that made up the iron framework were manufactured in a factory. They could be shipped anywhere, be bolted together at the site, and the glass panes slipped into place as the building went up. The resultant structure was light, yet strong. Furthermore, any part could be easily replaced if it became damaged.

Another brilliant example of structuring a metal framework in space was provided by the Eiffel Tower built in 1887 in Paris. While it was not planned specifically as architecture, its impact upon the thinking of architects was inevitable.

Modern high-rise architecture began in the United States when William Le Baron Jenney designed and built in 1885 the first steel skeleton building, a ten-story structure for the Home Insurance Company in Chicago. (Actually, iron was used for the first six stories and Bessemer steel beams for the remaining four levels.) With Jenney's breakthrough came the end of using thick and heavy outer walls to support the height and weight of a large building. Clearly, the stage was set for the emergence of the contemporary skyscraper.

Working from the ideas of Jenney, Louis Sullivan gave the skyscraper poetic form. He had little use for the reworked architectural fancy dress of the past. Instead, he dreamed of modern office towers, every inch proud and soaring. His famous phrase, "form follows function," became the battle cry of a new breed of architects and has continued to inspire his followers ever since.

ACTIVITIES TO EXPLORE:

1. Walk around your community and see if you can find examples of the following space-spanning devices inherited from the past: post and lintel construction, the round arch, dome, barrel vault, and the pointed arch.

2. Make a three-dimensional model of one of the great classic structures from the past such as the Parthenon, the Colosseum, the great Pyramid of Cheops, the Hagia Sophia or the Taj Mahal.

3. See what you can find out about how paintings and sculptures were used in conjunction with the architecture of the past. Share your findings with others in your art class.

4. Draw up a list of buildings in your community which you think will still be standing more than a hundred years from now. Then make another list of structures you feel will be gone from their site within the next fifty years. Be prepared to explain why you arrived at your conclusions.

5. Draw diagrams with a straightedge and a compass of the basic geometric shapes you find in the following structures from the past: Stonehenge, the great Pyramid of Cheops, the Parthenon, the Pantheon, the Colosseum, the Basilica of Saint Peter's and the cathedral of Notre Dame de Paris.

6. If you could go and see any one of the great buildings of yesteryear, which would you choose to visit? Why? Can you find out more about your choice by looking it up in the library?

Wright's best-known house and undoubtedly one of the
most beautiful residential designs of the twentieth century was built as a country retreat for the Edgar Kaufmann
family of Pittsburgh, Pennsylvania. Frank Lloyd Wright.
The Kaufmann House (Falling Water). Bear Run, Pennsylvania. 1937. (Photograph courtesy of Western Pennsylvania Conservancy, 204 Fifth Avenue, Pittsburgh,
Pennsylvania)

What is often called the modern style of architecture is not really a consistent style at all. Twentieth century architecture is a composite which reflects the diversified thinking of many different personalities. Unlike people working together in one community of thought, the greatest architects of our time have been intensely distinct individuals. Each evolved a personal style which, in time, became a source of inspiration for all architects.

Chapter Five

Great Milestones of Modern Architecture

Structures by Frank Lloyd Wright

Such ideas as open planning, blending the indoors and outdoors, and merging a structure with its site were among the valuable ideas pioneered by Frank Lloyd Wright in the early years of the twentieth century. He was also responsible for a host of innovations in the design of industrial architecture.

A very good example of his style is the country home he designed for the Edgar Kaufmann family of Pittsburgh, Pennsylvania. Called Falling Water because part of the house is projected in space over a waterfall, it has few equals insofar as functionality, nobility of concept, and sheer beauty are concerned.

The site for the house is the Bear Run Valley of Fayette County in western Pennsylvania. Wright was intrigued by the natural forest, massive sandstone boulders, free-flowing stream, native shrubbery, and Appalachian wildflowers. The key to the setting was the waterfall. As a central point of family activity, the Kaufmanns wanted the area around the falls as the location for their home.

Within its wooded setting, the house looks as though it grew out of the ground. The sense of unity between house and site is so vivid it can't be missed, even in a photograph. Everywhere you

33 Reaching upward, the tower forms a vertical counterpoint to the horizontal lines of the administration building. Frank Lloyd Wright. S. C. Johnson and Son Wax Company Research and Development Tower and Administration Building. Racine, Wisconsin. 1950. (Photograph courtesy of S. C. Johnson and Sons, Incorporated)

look, there is light, fresh air, atmosphere and space, all joined together.

In comparison with the Kaufmann house, consider Wright's design for the administration building and research and development tower of the S.C. Johnson and Son Company at Racine, Wisconsin. Together, the two structures house the company's central headquarters and laboratories.

Rising more than one hundred fifty feet into the air, the tower is fifty feet square. Each of the fifteen floors is cantilevered from a central core which, in turn, is anchored to a concrete foundation penetrating fifty-four feet into the earth. The foundation supports the central core in much the same way that a taproot supports the trunk of a tree. To follow that analogy further, the floors are like branches growing out from a tree trunk. The analogy ends where the outer shell of brick and glass serves as a protective sheath surrounding the tower, whereas trees have no such exterior curtain.

Hugging the ground, the nearby administration building forms a horizontal counterpoint to the vertical tower. Constructed in brick and glass, it was tailor-made for the specific needs of the Johnson's Wax Company. Wright has called the building an architectural interpretation of modern business at its best; it was designed, he said, "to be as inspiring a place in which to work as any cathedral ever was to worship in."

35 The combination of great strength, disciplined control of weight, and open spaces is clearly evident in the huge apartment house block built in Marseilles by Le Corbusier after World War II. Le Corbusier. Unité d'Habitation. Marseilles, France. 1947–1952. (Photograph by René Croebli, courtesy of the Pro Helvetia Foundation, Zurich, Switzerland)

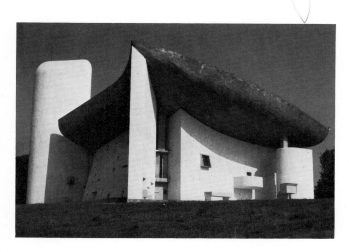

34 The rough stucco texture on the exterior walls of the church serves as an integrating force, unifying the assortment of shapes and windows that make up the total building. Le Corbusier. Chapel of Notre Dame du Haut. Ronchamp, France. 1950–1954. (Photograph by René Groebli, courtesy of the Pro Helvetia Foundation, Zurich, Switzerland)

Structures by Le Corbusier

In Europe, modern architects evolved an approach to design liberated from the ties to a local frame of reference. Therefore, quite logically, the new architectural vision of the twentieth century in Europe came to be called the International style. One of its most influential figures was the Swiss-born architect Charles Edouard Jeanneret, who adopted the name Le Corbusier (which, in French, means, "the builder").

In an apartment house (called the Unité d'Habitation) in southern France, Le Corbusier built a massive structure, poised in space atop a series of strong legs cast in concrete. Here, as in all his other commissions, the contrast of pale and dark shapes is alive with a rhythmic character all its own. By comparison, his poetically inspired chapel at Ronchamp is a triumph of designed lyricism. The solid walls, dotted with windows, become abstract patterns of light and shadow. The continuously fluid movement of the shapes takes your eyes on an exciting voyage through space. Even as you look at a black and white picture of the church, you find yourself thinking of such words as reason, elegance, simplicity, and freedom.

Besides feeling that modern buildings ought to be machines for living, Le Corbusier also believed the basic scale of a human being was the ideal unit of measurement upon which all architecture should be based. In short, he felt architectural forms should never become ends in themselves, should never lose touch with their social obligations, should always be concerned with rational solutions to environmental problems experienced by people in the pursuits of their everyday lives.

Structures by Ludwig Mies van der Rohe

Another major figure associated with the International style was Ludwig Mies van der Rohe. His achievements in glass and steel, such as the apartment houses he built on Lake Shore Drive in Chicago and New York City's Seagram Building are classic works of structural clarity stripped bare of any unnecessary ornamentation.

Students of architecture continue to repeat two of his most famous statements. The first, "less is more," suggests that the more one seeks to add what is needless, the less one is able to arrive at a solid sense of greatness in architecture. The other adage for which Mies (as he is generally called) has come to be remembered is the statement, "God is in the details," because it is the refinement and finesse of the Mies approach to detail that lends distinction to his work. Unfortunately, all too often, many of the people who copy his style fail to capture the quietly reserved elegance Mies was able to achieve.

Landmark Works of Exceptional Merit

Besides the accomplishments of such towering personalities as Wright, Le Corbusier, and Mies, there are certain distinguished examples of creative design by various other respected architects which deserve to be singled out for special notice. In their own way, each of them has proven to be highly valuable to the general development of the modern style.

For example, from the moment it was complete, the Pirelli Building has been important not only to the city of Milan, Italy, but also to architects all over the world. At a time when dull monotony threatened to make tall urban structures look bor-

36 Considering the cost of expensive midcity real estate, the use of half the building site for an open plaza was a daring departure from customary practice. Mies van der Rohe (in association with Philip C. Johnson). Seagram Building. New York, New York. 1958. (Photograph by Ezra Stoller, courtesy of Joseph E. Seagram and Sons, Incorporated)

37 Feelings of self-containment and soaring independence are among the most dominant qualities expressed by the design of the Pirelli Building. Gio Ponti (in association with Pier Luigi Nervi as structural engineer). Pirelli Building. Milan, Italy. 1958. (Photograph courtesy of Industrie Pirelli–S.p.A.)

38 The ground floor of this building includes an entrance lobby and open arcades on all sides; the offices are above on the mezzanine level. Mies van der Rohe. Bacardi Building. Mexico City, Mexico. 1961. (Photograph courtesy of Bacardi y Compañia, S.A.)

ingly repetitious, the Pirelli Building brought a bold and striking presence to the city scene. At any time of day or night, the massive height and shape of the building asserts itself so forcefully that the entire neighborhood where it is located stops being indifferent and commonplace.

Closer at hand, in the United States, the Richards Memorial Laboratories built for the medical school of the University of Pennsylvania is a group of towers reaching like fingers toward the sky. The various components of the building express the ever-changing light that comes and goes each day, crossing the face and body of the structure in an endless progression of patterns. To see those patterns is to become aware of the underlying rhythms of the whole world of nature.

39 The crisp-edged shapes of the building harmonize most agreeably with the organic nature of the site. Louis Kahn. Alfred Newton Richards Medical Research Building. Philadelphia, Pennsylvania. 1960. (Photograph by Lawrence Williams, Incorporated, courtesy of the University of Pennsylvania)

The city of Saint Louis, Missouri, has some of the most inspired works of architecture to be found anywhere. For example, there is the Gateway Arch, sheathed entirely in stainless steel and as tall as a sixty-two-story building. The arch was designed to commemorate the city that served as the jump-off point for the Lewis and Clark expedition and for many other westward-moving pioneers of the nineteenth century. While the parabolic shape of the arch may appear too fragile to withstand the force of a storm, it has stood up very well indeed since 1965 and is expected to continue doing so for years to come.

Close to the Gateway Arch is the Busch Memorial Stadium. Just as the arch is an updated version of ancient Roman commemorative arches, Busch Stadium is a dramatic twentieth-century treatment of the old Roman Sports arena called the Colosseum.

A third modern structure for which there is a historic ancestor is located at the Saint Louis-Lambert International Airport. The flight terminal building has arched vaults of thin concrete and glass that are reminiscent of the overhead vaults in ancient Roman bathhouses and civic structures.

Curving high above the ground, the arch is a graceful shape in space. Eero Saarinen. Gateway Arch. Saint Louis, Missouri. 1965. (Photograph by Ralph Walker, courtesy of the Missouri Tourism Commission and the Convention and Tourist Board of Greater Saint Louis)

41. The multipurpose stadium is one element of a huge civic
project in which thirty-four city blocks of urban blight
and decay were transformed into a dynamic new complex, housing various recreation and business enter-
prises. Edward Durell Stone. Busch Memorial Stadium.
Saint Louis, Missouri. 1966. (Photograph by Ralph Walker,
courtesy of the Missouri Tourism Commission and the
Convention and Tourist Board of Greater Saint Louis)

42 Cast concrete was the principal structural material used for the intersecting barrel-vaulted roof of this air terminal building. Minoru Yamasaki and Associates. Terminal Building, Lambert-Saint Louis International Airport. Saint Louis, Missouri. 1955. (Photograph courtesy of Weintraub and Associates)

43 People can move freely about the terminal interior since there are no obstructive upright verticals supporting the roof. Minoru Yamasaki and Associates. Terminal Building, Lambert-Saint Louis International Airport. Saint Louis, Missouri. 1955. (Photograph by Howard Earl Day, courtesy of Weintraub and Associates)

In designing headquarters for the Ford Foundation in New York City, the architects dealt with problems not solved by most office buildings. The conventional approach tends to isolate people, storing them away in cubicles with no sense of the working community to which they belong. In the Ford Foundation Building the design emerged as a C-shaped structure where people see each other frequently and which partially wraps around and shelters a large enclosed space. Inside this space there is a park, accessible to the public at large, complete with trees, shrubs, and flowering plants; a park where people may walk around and enjoy the greenery even in the middle of winter.

A visit to the City Hall of Toronto in Canada is an emotional experience of the highest order. By the power of its concept and the inspiring environment it provides for municipal government, it cannot help but affect the future development of the whole downtown central-city area in which it is located.

44 The great open space within the building, with many walkways accessible to the general public, is filled with lush greenery throughout the year. Kevin Roche. Ford Foundation Building. New York, New York. 1967. (Photograph by ESTO for the Ford Foundation, courtesy of the Ford Foundation Office of Reports)

45 The significance of the Toronto City Hall is boldly expressed in shapes rarely seen in many large cities. Viljo Revell. Toronto City Hall. Toronto, Canada. 1965. (Photograph by the Toronto Fire Department, courtesy of the City of Toronto, Canada)

Cast in concrete, the roof over the Opera House of Sidney, Australia, consists of shapes based upon great curved slices of spheres. At first glance, they seem to rise like praying hands or sails on a floating craft. Of course, much of the excitement generated by the structure is due to its location. Surrounded by water and the endless sweep of sky overhead, the building is as much an abstract piece of sculpture as it is a functional space where audiences may enjoy musical performances.

Three other futuristic buildings appear to point to the path many architects of tomorrow may choose to follow.

Marina City in Chicago is a pair of cylindrical towers, sixty stories high. The first eighteen levels of each unit are parking garages. The remaining levels serve as space for offices, restaurants, and residences. The apartment house floors, cantilevered from the central stem, are reminiscent of the cantilevered floors in the Johnson's Wax Company Research and Development Tower at Racine, Wisconsin.

The sixty-story-high First National Bank of Chicago is also a distinctive building because of its upswept sides. The building stands out from its surroundings not only because it is unusually high but also because it is located upon a beautifully landscaped plaza.

46 The repeating shapes in the twin cylinders generate a twisting rising rhythm unduplicated by any other structure ever built anywhere. Bertram Goldberg and Associates. Marina City, Chicago, Illinois. 1964. (Photograph courtesy of the City of Chicago, Department of Development and Planning)

In a close-up view, the upswept curvature of the building may be more fully appreciated than when the structure is seen from a distance. C. F. Murphy and the Perkins and Will Partnership. The First National Bank of Chicago. Chicago, Illinois. 1964. (Photograph by Oscar and Associates, courtesy of the First National Bank of Chicago)

The opera house shells present a flight of architectural fancy, quite unique in the world. Jørn Utzon. Sydney Opera House. Sydney, Australia. 1972. (Photograph courtesy of the Australian Information Service)

49 Fuller's dome construction suggests a vast range of possible applications that have yet to be fully explored and utilized. Buckminster Fuller. The Climatron. Saint Louis, Missouri. 1960. (Photograph by Ralph Walker, courtesy of the Missouri Tourism Commission and the Convention and Tourist Board of Greater Saint Louis)

According to many architectural authorities, the geodesic dome of Buckminster Fuller, which makes use of simple module elements for spanning space, is one of the most important design developments of the contemporary period. Constructed with strong lightweight materials, the segments can be used to cover a wide range of volumes. A good example of the geodesic dome in actual use is the Climatron at the Botanical Garden in Saint Louis. The huge greenhouse was the first structure of its kind to be enclosed in shatterproof transparent plastic panels. To date, no other architect has invented a single universal unit that can be successfully applied to so many different demands for providing a protective shelter in which walls and roof combine into one continuously flowing, surprisingly sturdy, all-encompassing form.

Of course, no one today can predict with absolute accuracy what further changes will take place in the architecture of tomorrow. For example, the size and location of future populations will have to be taken into account by architects as they proceed with their work. Likewise, the potentials of mass production and prefabrication technology have yet to be fully realized. Naturally, creative architects are aware of these possibilities and are doing all they can to use them in their designs. Considering what has been accomplished to date, there is good reason to believe the last quarter of the twentieth century will be even brighter architecturally than the previous three quarters have been.

ACTIVITIES TO EXPLORE:

1. Make a series of sketches of the most interesting modern buildings you can find in your community. Try to capture how the structures "feel" in your drawings.

2. Can you find any evidence of inventive thought in the new buildings that have been erected where you live? Explain to other people in your class what difference inventiveness makes in the appearance of a modern building.

3. Make a visual catalog of the different patterns you observed in the newly built structures you found in your community.

4. Can you find buildings where you live that appear to have structural and visual characteristics similar to the examples discussed in this chapter? For example, consider such factors as cantilevering, use of glass, poured concrete and steel, freedom from excessive ornamentation, and the presence of unusual three-dimensional shapes.

5. Project plans on paper for a large office building. Take into account the materials and construction techniques that would be necessary for your design to become a reality.

6. Analyze a structure you know, such as your school, to find its shortcomings. If you could redesign it, what changes would you make in order to improve the functional efficiency and appearance of this building?

51 The arrow striking the center of the bison suggests a magic wish-fulfillment purpose for the picture. Rendered with great sensitivity, the profile view painted with a contour outline is highly naturalistic in appearance. Bison from the caves at Lascaux (Dordogne), France. About 15,000–10,000 B.C. (Photograph courtesy of French Embassy Press and Information Division, 972 Fifth Avenue, New York, New York)

50 The abstract figure composition, rich with repeating patterns and stylized shapes, has a timeless look. The hieroglyphic elements complement the large seated forms. Wall painting from the Tomb of Queen Nefertiti at Thebes (Luxor), Egypt. (Photograph by Sobhi Afifi, courtesy of the Egyptian Government Tourist Office, New York, New York)

Long before any written records were kept, people left evidence of their existence in the form of paintings on cave walls. Quite possibly, that is when art first began.

The Ancient World

The painted images on cave walls suggest the ancient cave dwellers were probably hunters. Perhaps the pictures were made as some kind of supernatural insurance. If the human hand could capture the essence of an animal and fix it in place on a wall, then perhaps an actual animal would follow suit and fall to the human hands using an arrow, rock, club, or spear.

Possibly, the idea of putting animal images on a wall deep within the earth was also meant as a fertility ritual, the painting act serving in some sort of magical way to insure the continued presence of animals. Such animals could then be hunted in order to provide the cave dwellers with food and warm coverings.

In those days, an artist could not walk into an art supply store and buy jars and tubes of paint and artist's tools. Instead, all supplies were made by hand. Grinding rocks and different colors of earth into a fine powder provided the basic pigments. The raw colors were then probably mixed with animal fat (oil in that bygone era) or vegetable gums (watercolor) and applied with such rude implements as twigs, hollow reeds, fingertips, stones, bits of fur, and animal claws.

By comparison with the earthy art of the Stone Age, filled with naturalistic forms reflecting a knowledge of animal anatomy and movement, the paintings of historic Egypt are remarkably sophisticated, rich with highly stylized forms, and composed with

Chapter Six

The Art of Painting

52 A beautifully balanced abstraction of historic figures, this mosaic design has successfully survived more than fourteen centuries since it was first created. *Empress Theodora and Her Court*. Mosaic in the Church of San Vitale at Ravenna, Italy. sixth century A.D. (Photograph by S. D. Anderson, courtesy of Alinari)

53 Intertwining forms and a repeating range of tones cause the different elements of this design to become a solidly unified arrangement. Wall paintings in fresco medium from the Villa of the Mysteries. Pompeii, Italy. first century A.D. (Photograph by S. D. Anderson, courtesy of Alinari)

an eye keenly aware of decorative arrangement. In large measure, the painters of early Egypt repeated forms according to an established formula, carefully avoiding any drift toward free personal expression. The images they created have a timeless character, capable of enduring through the ages.

Later Developments

Unfortunately, there are no remains of wall painting from the golden age of ancient Greece. Instead, what we have today from that period twenty-five hundred years ago are fascinating images made on clay vessels in all sizes and shapes. The pottery pictures are elaborate with detail involving the life of the gods as well as the day-to-day experiences of ordinary people on earth.

Going on to the time of ancient Rome, we do find remnants of wall paintings done in that era. These paintings offer a good idea of how the ancient Romans liked to decorate the interiors of their homes and other buildings. The paintings were frequently done in fresco, which consists of applying paint to a fresh plaster surface while it is still moist. The pigments become incorporated in the plaster as it dries and thus they don't scale or chip off as colors might if they were only on the surface. For that reason, the hues and tones of the old Roman fresco paintings are almost as clear and bright today as when they were first brushed on to the walls over fifteen hundred years ago.

In addition to painted ornamentation, the ancient Romans also used mosaic decorations on their floors and walls. The practice of making mosaics probably originated with the ancient Greeks, and the Romans adapted what they learned from their immediate predecessors. A mosaic consists of many thousands of tiny multicolored chips of glass, stone, or ceramicware cemented to a surface, forming a picture or design.

After the fall of the Roman Empire, the practice of painting on walls went into decline. What little painting did take place was done mostly in hand-lettered books that were copied by monks from the Bible and the ancient classics. Nevertheless, a modest amount of wall painting from the early medieval era can also be found today in the crypts of certain old churches of the period. As one might expect, they tend to be concerned only with religious subject matter.

Lively decorative figures animate the miniature mural composition wrapped around this piece of pottery. Like a fine lace network, the linear details harmonize with the silhouette shapes. *Black-Figured Krater.* By an Attic artist from the archaic period (560–550 B.C.). Ceramicware. Greece. Collection of the Dallas (Texas) Museum of Fine Arts; Gift of the Jonsson Foundation, and Mr. and Mrs. Frederick M. Mayer. (Photograph by D. Widmer, courtesy of the Dallas Museum of Fine Arts)

As the Roman Empire faded into history, a new stylistic development came with the emergence of the Byzantine period. Typically, Byzantine art has a flat decorative style. By and large, figures are treated in a symbolic manner, to suggest divine images rather than earthly presences. The visual forms reflect the strength and authority exercised at the time by the Church. The flat handling of paint may also have been motivated by a desire to discard the pagan influences of the ancient Greeks and Romans who had projected a highly representational approach to their creative work in two and three dimensions.

Toward the end of the medieval era, a new approach to art gradually evolved in the West. With the building of the new Gothic cathedrals in the twelfth and thirteenth centuries, there gradually arose a need for paintings dealing with religious subject matter which could be used for ornamental and instructional purposes inside a church.

The flattened shapes seen here suggest a spiritual existence in heaven rather than a picture of earthbound physical realities. *Enthroned Madonna and Child.* Byzantine. Tempera and gold leaf on wooden panel; thirteenth century A.D. National Gallery of Art, Washington, D.C.; Andrew Mellon Collection

Though Christ and Mary are divine personages, they appear in Giotto's painting as a natural (rather than supernatural) mother and child. Giotto. *Madonna and Child*. Tempera and gold leaf on wood; about 1300. National Gallery of Art, Washington, D.C.; Samuel H. Kress Collection.

The Renaissance

At the end of the fifteenth century, there was a tremendous growth and development of painting throughout Europe. Many princes, bankers, and wealthy merchants of the period invited artists to make paintings for use as decorations in their homes and palaces. They felt they could enjoy the same richness and beauty as the churches had commissioned before them.

In southern Europe, especially in Italy, an emphasis was placed on life in the present and also upon the appearance of real people. One of the most gifted artists of the Early Renaissance, as this period came to be called, was Giotto. Increasingly, he humanized the image of figures in his work. Soon, virtually all the other artists of the time were follwing his lead.

Besides changes in the treatment of subject matter, the Renaissance saw significant developments take place in the technical side of the painter's craft. Of course, the fresco technique continued to be widely used. In addition, painters also made panel-size pieces using a tempera medium made of egg yolk (which served as a permanent binder) mixed with water and finely ground pigments in varied colors. However, the newest medium that began to be used more and more was oil, by itself or in combination with resin varnishes. At first, the colors ground in oil were applied as transparent glazes over underlayers painted in egg-tempera. Eventually, oils were used without tempera, in as many layers as were necessary to develop the fullest richness, detail, depth, and luminosity sought by the artists. At roughly the same time, in the early sixteenth century, canvas replaced wood as the most widely used support for paintings since fabric

was easier to handle, especially for large-size works. In addition, canvas stretched tightly on a lightweight frame was more stable than wood, which tended to split and develop stresses due to temperature and humidity changes in the atmosphere.

Some of the earliest work in oil was done by the Flemish artists Hubert and Jan Van Eyck during the fifteenth century. Gradually, all the potentials of the medium were explored, from liquid veils of very thin color, through translucent notes of scumbled brush strokes, to the heavy-bodied deposits of impasto, or thick pasty pileups of paint on a surface. To the present day, painters still use these three basic ways of applying oils to a surface.

57 While at prayer, the Virgin Mary is advised by the Archangel Gabriel that she will give birth to Christ. The lily flowers in the foreground symbolize her purity, while a dove descending on a beam of light represents the presence of God. Jan van Eyck. *The Annunciation*. Oil, originally on wood, now transferred to canvas; between 1425 and 1440. National Gallery of Art, Washington, D.C.; Andrew Mellon Collection.

ACTIVITIES TO EXPLORE:

1. Make believe you are an ancient cave painter. Make a picture of animals with tempera paints, but instead of using brushes, use any other tools you can find such as sticks, cloth, leaves, or bits of fur.

2. Suppose you want to paint but there is no place where you can buy ready-mixed colors. What would you do? Can you think of ways to make paints from natural materials that are readily available?

3. Think of your contacts with other people and develop some sketches in which the human relationships you've thought about become the central focus of your pictures. Select the best sketch and make it into a painting.

4. For thousands of years, people have used art to express their deepest beliefs about religion. Can you make a vividly expressive image in which the faith you believe in is given form in paint?

5. Take time to look at the artwork of some young children. Talk with them about the picture they've made and try to understand what they wanted to express.

6. If you live near an art museum with a collection of old paintings, go into the galleries there and examine the difference between paintings done in traditional egg-tempera medium and those done in oil. As you look at the work on view, ask yourself what difference the medium makes in the appearance of the pictures.

58 Sensitive refinement, deep concentration, and polite modesty have all been superbly captured in van der Weyden's portrait study. The face of the figure, framed by a triangle of transparent veiling, glows with inner radiance as pale shades of color vibrate quietly beside opaque darks. Rogier van der Weyden. *Portrait of a Lady*. Oil on wood; about 1455. National Gallery of Art, Washington, D.C.; Andrew Mellon Collection.

59   By the use of *chiaroscuro* (an Italian word referring to the
      interplay of light and shadow), Leonardo was able to
      model solid forms in space, suggest distance, and bring
      different colors into harmony with each other. In this
      example, the compelling sadness and dignified nobility of
      the portrait tell as much about the universal nature of the
      human condition as they reveal about the subject and
      her personality. Leonardo da Vinci. *Portrait of Ginevra de
      Benci.* Oil on wood panel; about 1480. National Gallery
      of Art, Washington, D.C.; Ailsa Mellon Bruce Fund.

By the middle of the sixteenth century, the arts were flourishing in the Western world. Never before had so many creative personalities dedicated themselves to achieving the highest possible levels of quality in their work.

Chapter Seven

Painting: Between the Ancient Past and the Present

The Renaissance

Of all the artists associated with the Renaissance, few could equal the accomplishments of Leonardo da Vinci and Michelangelo Buonarroti. While they sought to carry out the requirements of specific commissions (such as religious subjects or portraits), they also evolved personal styles that were uniquely their own. Each wanted to be more than just a competent craftsman working at a trade. Compared with the anonymous artisan of the medieval era, they felt a profound need to express their own intellectual and emotional commitments in the forms they composed with color and line. Refusing to be simple picture makers, they elevated the painter's role to a level formerly reserved only for poets, philosophers, and mathematicians; thus they took painting from the plane of the mechanical to the liberal arts.

Starting with the Renaissance, a new scientific outlook, based upon objective experimentation, began to emerge. Leonardo da Vinci lived at the beginning of this new era. His observations and experiments contributed significantly to its development. But most of all, by instinct as well as by training, Leonardo was an artist. For him, vision was the key to all knowledge, because seeing is the basic instrument of human perception. By means of his art, Leonardo was able to project new ideas and illustrate principles which could not be easily explained in words.

The thoroughness of his early studies combined with a great natural curiosity and great powers of intellectual speculation led Leonardo to become the perfect model of the Renaissance man, a person of many talents, competent in the study of life and the pursuit of the arts as well as the sciences. Certainly that would explain why his paintings have such a timeless universality about them. In Leonardo's work, light and shade were used to create space, envelop form, suggest distance, lend harmony to variations of color, and sometimes serve as the very basis of the painting itself. With a masterful hand, he was able to combine profound psychological insights with a reverence for nature that eloquently expresses the human pursuit of ideals.

Michelangelo, the other great genius of the Italian Renaissance, was in many ways the very opposite of Leonardo because he took almost no interest in science. As an artist, he was not a calm observer, recording things objectively, but a creative personality in whose hands inanimate materials suddenly came to life. Michelangelo's huge fresco covers the entire ceiling of the Sistine Chapel. Working as much as eighteen hours a day for four years, Michelangelo painted images illustrating stories from the Bible, the lives of various prophets, and even characters from ancient mythology.

One of the most extraordinary sections of the ceiling is the panel in which Michelangelo dealt with the creation of Adam. The figure of God the Father rushing through the sky is nothing less than the source of all creative energy in the universe. Adam, in contrast, still clings to the earth from which he was molded. The hands of Adam and God reach out toward each other and almost touch. Suddenly, life is generated as static matter turns into a dynamic presence.

The Baroque

Constantly seeking to refresh and advance the language of vision, creative painters are not content to simply repeat the past. And so, as the sixteenth century gave way to the seventeenth, the world of art moved out of the Renaissance and into a new period called the Baroque.

A major figure of the new style was the Flemish artist Peter Paul Rubens. As a young man, he spent eight years in Italy studying the works of the great painters of the Renaissance. However, more important than the classical foundation of his training were the personal vitality and creative resourcefulness he brought to painting.

In Rubens's work, everything is always alive. Swirling movement sweeps through every picture. In addition to his own efforts with brush in hand, Rubens also maintained a painting factory where various artists of considerable ability worked on his pictures. That fact explains why many of the paintings attributed today to Rubens were actually done as much by other painters as by Rubens himself. And yet, Rubens receives the credit for them because he conceived the compositions initially. He thoroughly supervised their execution, his eye always checking, approving or disapproving what was done by the craftsmen who worked out the details.

While other gifted artists lived during the seventeenth century, few can bear comparison with Rembrandt van Rijn, probably the greatest Dutch painter of the Baroque period. Between 1633 and 1642, it was the height of fashion for wealthy people in Amsterdam to have their portraits painted by him. However, as he grew older, Rembrandt became less and less interested in worldly success. Instead, he became increasingly concerned with the

Michelangelo's deep feeling for human life, his dramatic ideas, and his religion made his ceiling of the Sistine Chapel one of the greatest paintings of all time. In this panel, where the divine spark of life reaches Adam, inanimate matter is suddenly changed from molded clay into moving flesh and blood. Equally important is the image of Eve, still unborn, protected by the Lord's left arm, looking toward the man with whom she will share her life on earth. Michelangelo Buonarrotti. *The Creation of Adam*. From the ceiling of the Sistine Chapel. Vatican City, Rome, Italy. Fresco; 1508–1512. (Photograph by S. D. Anderson, courtesy of Alinari)

The turbulent drama, typical of work by Rubens, is clearly evident in this example. Peter Paul Rubens. *Daniel in the Lion's Den*. c.1615. National Gallery of Art, Washington, D. C.; Ailsa Mellon Bruce Fund.

84

62 The complexities of physical change and spiritual growth are suggested with disarming candor in Rembrandt's *Self-Portrait.* Few painters have ever equaled his depth and power of expression. Rembrandt van Rijn. *Self-Portrait.* Oil on canvas; 1659. National Gallery of Art, Washington, D.C.; Andrew Mellon Collection.

drama of life as it may be revealed emotionally and intellectually in a language of art. Involving himself with great universal themes, he invented relationships of light and dark to express the depths of human feeling with paint on canvas. His self-portraits provide an especially good example of the deep concern he felt for the analysis and interpretation of human experience.

During the eighteenth century, the Baroque style underwent a change of approach that came to be called the Rococo. The new style was concerned with being decorative and pretty. As a typical example of the Rococo period, an artist such as Jean Fragonard would paint pictures of people at court enjoying themselves, completely unmindful of anything except their own pleasure.

63 Luxuriating in lighthearted amusement, the people of Fragonard's outdoor setting are obviously enjoying themselves. The picture, filled with floating grace and airy splendor, is an elegant example of the Rococo style. Jean Honoré Fragonard. *The Swing.* Oil on canvas; c.1765s. National Gallery of Art, Washington, D.C.; Samuel H. Kress Collection.

The Nineteenth Century

After the French and American revolutions took place at the end of the eighteenth century, the nineteenth century witnessed the emergence of a new social order. Gradually, the middle class replaced the monarchy as the main source of authority.

As the middle class took more and more control, changes also took place in the field of painting. Some were minor — merely shifts of emphasis in subject matter or variations in painting techniques. Such changes were more changes of fashion than changes of substance. On the other hand, there were painters who brought about major changes in creative expression because they abandoned the accepted practices of traditional academic art.

By and large, academic art emphasized the use of distinctive outlines, balanced compositions, smoothly modeled figures, muted coloring, and what the academicians called "noble expression", which meant historical, religious, or mythological subjects for their paintings. By contrast, the new Romantic style, exemplified by the work of Delacroix, involved the use of rich hues and live action to express some emotionally stirring narrative.

The romantic story of Columbus and his early difficulties come alive in this picture. Here Delacroix depicts the dramatic moment just before the explorer suddenly learns his proposals have won favor and he will finally be able to embark on his historic voyage of discovery. Euguène Delacroix. *Columbus and His Son at La Rabida*. Oil on canvas; 1838. National Gallery of Art, Washington, D.C.; Chester Dale Collection.

Another direction that emerged during the middle of the nineteenth century came to be called Realism because such artists as Daumier in France and Eakins in America concerned themselves with subject matter based upon realities they observed in life. Their simple vocabulary of form looked and felt very different from either Romanticism or Academism.

In the third quarter of the nineteenth century, another new style, Impressionism, emerged at approximately the same time the Industrial Revolution was taking place. The artists associated with Impressionism used color for the sake of expressing their experience with light and atmosphere. Making use of a very spontaneous approach, they drew upon direct contact with nature as the main source of their inspiration. Their paints, applied with a sensitive touch, caught the fleeting moment, suggesting how subjects looked when seen with the freshness of sudden discovery. The great masters of Impressionism whose works continue to enjoy great respect and widespread favor today were Claude Monet, Pierre Auguste Renoir, and Edgar Degas.

Following the Impressionists, there was another development which, in time, came to be called Post-Impressionism. However, it was more than an art movement with basic characteristics shared in common by several different painters. Post-Impressionism comprised the work of highly individualistic artists who were all intensely different from each other in their approach to art.

65 The representation of solid form in space is accomplished here by the controlled interplay of light and shadow. Honoré Daumier. *Advice to a Young Artist.* Oil on canvas; 1855–1860. National Gallery of Art, Washington, D.C.; Gift of Duncan Phillips.

66 Situated between the water and the land, the two figures provide a double focus, tying all the different shapes of the composition together into a unified whole. The repeating pattern of horizontal shapes lends further authority to the picture's sense of balance. Thomas Eakins. *The Biglin Brothers Racing.* Oil on canvas; c.1873. National Gallery of Art, Washington, D.C.; Presented by Mr. and Mrs. Cornelius Vanderbilt Whitney.

67 A fleeting moment in time is captured forever in the shimmering glow of ballet dancers twisting and turning in space. Edgar Degas. *Ballet Scene.* Pastel; c. 1907. National Gallery of Art, Washington, D.C.; Chester Dale Collection.

68 Refusing to let his brush function as a cold camera lens, van Gogh painted every canvas he touched with an intensity of subjective feeling. Vincent van Gogh. *La Mousmé.* Oil on canvas; 1888. National Gallery of Art, Washington, D.C.; Chester Dale Collection.

69 Harmony and equilibrium are evident throughout every square inch of Cézanne's landscape. Each touch of color is essential. Anything unnecessary has been carefully excluded. Paul Cézanne. *Landscape in Provence.* Oil on canvas; c. 1880. National Gallery of Art, Washington, D.C.; Chester Dale Collection.

70 Luminous colors, handsomely woven together, have been transformed into a bewitching picture of a little girl. The delicate tones, textures, and varied shapes spread over the canvas surface, producing a flow of gentle movements filled with infinite tenderness and peace. Pierre August Renoir. *Girl with a Hoop.* Oil on canvas; 1885. National Gallery of Art, Washington, D.C.; Chester Dale Collection.

Probably the best-known of all of the Post-Impressionists was the Dutch artist Vincent van Gogh. He breathed such life into his colors they still jolt our sensibilities and attract our attention whenever we see them. The intensity of his feelings, throbbing with nervous energy in heavy, built-up layers of paint, is clearly evident in every one of his pictures. Furthermore, we never mistake his paintings for those of another artist because they are so distinctively his.

Working alone in southern France, Paul Cézanne, another of the great Post-Impressionists, devoted himself to creating a new way of dealing with form and space on a two-dimensional surface. Using simplified shapes and bold colors, he evolved a system of applying many short strokes of paint side by side until they all fused together into a grand and monumental design. He would transform his perceptions of the three-dimensional world into a highly organized composition that never compromised the truth of the flat canvas surface. As a visual experience, it proved to be an extraordinary breakthrough.

Perhaps more than any other artist of the late nineteenth century, Cézanne asserted the need for art to express a reality of its own instead of merely imitating the reality of objects existing outside the artwork. For that reason, he is generally regarded as one of the great fathers of several new movements that emerged in the art world during the years following his death, early in the twentieth century.

When the Impressionists and Post-Impressionists first exhibited their work, visitors were often shocked. Their lack of familiarity with forms they had never seen before made them feel uneasy. They often reacted with anger, and, instead of seeking to learn more about the new art of their time, they attacked it with ridicule. Apparently, what seemed terribly radical to so many people back then looks rather tame today. Perhaps there is an important lesson to be drawn from these facts. When we have occasion to confront unfamiliar art forms, we should not rush to judgment until we have taken time to really find out what the work is about. Otherwise, we may cheat ourselves out of art experiences that might have been very satisfying and meaningful.

ACTIVITIES TO EXPLORE:

1. In what ways did the painters of the past fulfill functions carried out today by still photography, cinema, and television?

2. As you consider the history of painting from the Renaissance to the end of the nineteenth century, can you find reasons to account for the great stylistic shifts that have taken place over the years?

3. Which painters of the past excite your interest? Why?

4. When you look at art from yesteryear, what does the work tell you about the time in which it was produced? Give specific examples.

5. In what ways does a knowledge of certain creative personalities of the past, such as Leonardo da Vinci, Michelangelo, and Rembrandt, make a difference in your life? Would you be the same person you are now if you had never heard of them and their work?

6. From the pictures reproduced in this chapter, choose the ones that appeal to you the most. Then explain the reasons for your selections.

The sparkle and freshness of transparent watercolor handled by a master of the medium is immediately apparent in this picture. John Marin. *New York, 1925.* Watercolor; 1925. Collection of the Philadelphia Museum of Art. (Photograph by A. J. Wyatt, Staff Photographer)

Often, the first impression of modern painting many people have is one of enormous variety and complexity. However, if the years since 1900 are carefully studied, certain patterns of development can be identified; the overall period revealing itself as a network of interacting causes, influences, and effects. This may help to explain why there is such a variety of art forms today.

The modern era has been especially fertile for scientists, inventors, and explorers. They have explored vast areas of human concern ranging all the way from the interior of the brain to the outermost limits of the known universe. Like their counterparts in the scientific community, many modern artists have also pioneered new ways of creating expressive form to a degree unequaled in any former period of history.

While most serious paintings since the turn of the century have been done in oils, modern artists have also made extensive use of watercolor. Unlike oils, which tend to be treated rather deliberately, watercolor can be used in a spontaneous fashion. Absolute control is rarely possible with this fluid medium. More often than not, watercolor on a wet surface is unpredictable. The painter must be prepared to make the most of chance "accidents" that unfold as the washes of liquid pigment flow into and over each other. An oil won't grow "stale" when a painting problem arises calling for a study of possible alternatives to resolve the difficulty. However, as a rule, watercolor doesn't permit such luxury. Decisions about what to do at a particular stage in a picture's development must be made immediately, while the colors are still wet. After they dry, one cannot go back over them again without losing the sparkle and vitality implicit in the medium.

Chapter Eight

Painting in the Modern Age

The heartbeat of a city comes alive in the turbulent movement of Eisenstat's Expressionist vision. This picture tingles with an impulsive nervous rhythm common to urban scenes. Ben Eisenstat. *South on Broad.* Acrylic emulsion on composition board; 1973. (Photograph courtesy of the artist)

Another painting medium that has come to be more and more widely used since the 1950s is the plastic emulsion medium. Entirely new synthetic paints, generally made of polymerized acrylic resin emulsions and finely ground pigment, they permit a combination of traditional oil and watercolor techniques. Mixed with water, the polymer emulsion colors can be applied in thin transparent washes as in classical watercolor techniques. At the same time (and in the same painting), it is possible to use them in a thick paste consistency as with oil paints squeezed from a tube.

For practical purposes, there is no single movement or direction we can identify as modern art. Instead, as we look back, we find various schools of thought taking shape. Because the characteristics typical of any particular style are shared by all the artists pursuing that approach, it may be useful here to describe the various major movements that have emerged since the turn of the century.

Fauvism and Expressionism

The first distinctively new painting approach to appear in the twentieth century was promptly given the derogatory name Fauvism. The term was coined by a critic who wished to suggest that artists associated with this direction were painting as though they were wild animals (which is what the word "fauves" means in French). The painters identified with Fauvism emphasized the use of simplified flat areas filled with intense color to get and sustain bold ideas in paint.

Expressionism, still widely pursued as a painting style, first appeared in Germany and in the early work of Pablo Picasso at approximately the same time Fauvism was making headway in France. In

73 Foremost among the Fauve painters, Matisse explored new ways of using simplified shapes and intense colors in his work. Henri Matisse. *The Moorish Screen.* Oil on canvas; 1922. Collection of the Philadelphia Museum of Art; Bequest of Lisa Norris Elkins.

common with the Fauve painters, the Expressionists took much of their initial inspiration from the art of van Gogh, Cézanne, and other Post-Impressionists.

Both movements aimed to create forms which would unlock an artist's innermost feelings and spread them out on canvas where they could then be shared with people, openly and honestly. Distortion was used freely to heighten the emotional impact a painting might make. This explains why their pictures often touch the heart as well as the eye of a spectator.

Cubism

While Cubism was a logical extension of Cézanne's creative thought, it was also the most dramatic twentieth-century break from the old picture-making traditions of the art world. Cubism was invented when artists transformed the way they saw a subject into an orderly abstraction made of flat shapes. The resulting design would take on a character and life of its own, no longer trying to be an imitation or photograph of the original subject. It was not long before other artists followed suit, and all manner of variations in abstract form have appeared ever since.

Besides extending the artist's horizon of expression, the Cubists also enlarged the technical vocabulary of the painter when they introduced collage in their work. A collage is made by attaching pieces of material to a flat background. Typically, background supports are paper, cardboard, canvas, plastic, wood, or metal. Often, collage elements are combined with paints. Pure collages and combinations of collage and paint have been made from such varied materials as colored paper, newsprint, railway tickets, photographs, old engravings, pieces of

The atmosphere of a busy street can be felt in the merged layers of paint and pasted paper. An especially strong sense of depth results from the overlapping of various materials on the surface. Ruth Petlock. *Fun City.* Collage and acrylic polymer emulsion paint on plywood; 1973. Collection of Doctors June and Sol Nemzof. (Photograph by John H. Busser, Jr., courtesy of the artist)

Three costumed figures and their musical instruments
have been transformed into an abstraction of flat shapes
and repeating patterns. Pablo Picasso. *Three Musicians*.
Oil on canvas; 1921. A. E. Gallatin Collection; Philadelphia Museum of Art. (Photograph by A. J. Wyatt, Staff
Photographer)

Primary colors vibrating with excitement have been composed here in a highly disciplined arrangement. Stuart Davis. *Something on the Eight Ball*. Oil on canvas; 1954. Collection of the Philadelphia Museum of Art.

string, hair, and fabric. Since the early Cubists first introduced collage, it has been widely used by artists moving in many different directions seeking visual richness in their work.

Nonrepresentational Abstraction

When the Cubists eliminated the obvious appearance of subject matter, focusing instead on new ways of creating a designed sense of order, some artists felt an impulse to go further and discard subject matter entirely. Thus, they would be free to concentrate completely on absolutely pure forms. For many, the invention of metaphors embodying spiritual and material perfection is a main goal. Others have developed a language of subjective vision called Abstract Expressionism. A third approach sometimes called Op Art involves images rich in optical kinetic action. The dazzling patterns of this latter trend have also found many applications outside of painting, in textiles, on wallcoverings, and for commercial art of all kinds.

Fantastic Art and Surrealism

One of the most influential currents running through the river of modern art comes from the universal human capacity for projecting fanciful pictures out of the imagination. Frequently, such fantasy images are drawn from dreams. They often look like hand-painted snapshots, illustrating episodes no camera could ever capture because no camera can ever enter the center of a person's brain where dreams actually take place.

There is no end to the possible associations suggested by Fantastic Art and Surrealism (a French word for the superreality perceived by all the senses working together on a subconscious as well

Transparent veils of intense color drift weightlessly across the surface of Louis's canvas. Morris Louis. *Beth.* Acrylic resin on canvas; 1960. Collection of the Philadelphia Museum of Art.

Liberated from all reference to objects, Kandinsky's painting is an example of absolutely pure nonrepresentational form. Wassily Kandinsky. *Little Painting with Yellow.* Oil on canvas; 1914. Collection of the Philadelphia Museum of Art.

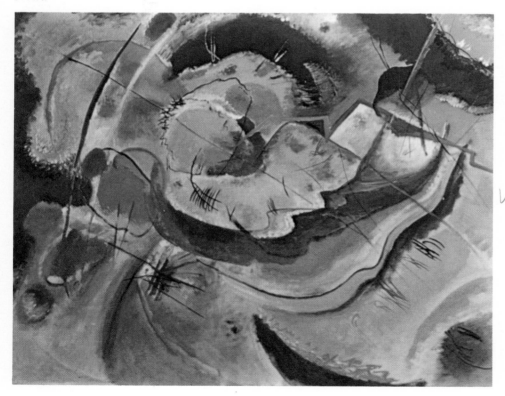

as conscious level of experience). On occasion, the forms in these pictures seem very familiar. At other times they are remote and peculiarly bizarre. But invariably, they are fascinating and appealing.

Social Criticism

The deep concern of the Expressionists for exercising their emotional sensitivities and giving them a visual voice fathered the outgrowth of modern social commentary in paint. For example, at the time of World War I, a movement called Dada sprang into existence as an outcry against the barbarism of armed hostility and the excesses of technology directed against people. Today, many painters, working more as independent individuals than as members of a unified art group, use paint to speak out against injustice, cruelty, and unfair exploitation practiced against defenseless human beings. For that reason, images of people in desperate circumstances often appear as the main focus of their work.

Pop Art

Filling the gap between the purity of nonrepresentational art and the earthy facts of life treated by the Social Realists is the movement called Pop Art. This new direction makes use of such popular (therefore, "pop") sources of visual form as street signs, printed pictures, comic strips, and package designs.
    Generally speaking, the Pop approach consists of discovering unexpected possibilities for interpretation and expression in subject matter usually thought to be inappropriate for such purposes. Pop artists put their audience in close touch with bits and pieces of the everyday world that are usually

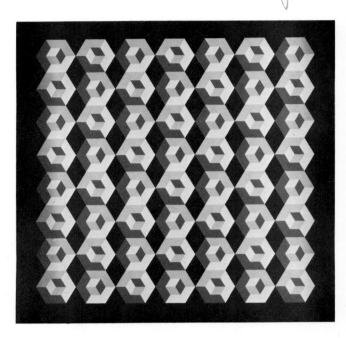

79 The repeating shapes seem to constantly change as variations in color and tone transform the flat hexagons into actively moving blocklike solids. Edna Andrade. *Hot Blocks*. Oil on canvas; 1966–1967. Collection of the Philadelphia Museum of Art. (Photograph by A. J. Wyatt, Staff Photographer)

80 Like seeing page after page in a news magazine or watching successive images flash across a TV screen, the composite of pictures and moving paint action invite your eye to participate in an exciting voyage of visual discovery. Robert Rauschenberg. *Estate*. Oil and printer's ink on canvas; 1963. Collection of the Philadelphia Museum of Art. (Photograph by A. J. Wyatt, Staff Photographer)

81 The brooding sadness of the foreground figure expresses a profound sense of suffering. All the other details support the general theme of bitterness and grief. Ben Shahn. *Miners' Wives*. Tempera; 1948. Collection of the Philadelphia Museum of Art.

82 Possessing a rich imagination, Klee projected a flow of playful forms, done with a light touch and a hint of childlike whimsy. Paul Klee. *Landscape with Three Bluebirds*. Watercolor on chalk-primed canvas; 1919. Collection of the Philadelphia Museum of Art.

overlooked. Because the commonplace objects are transformed into artworks through the magic of painting, they take on new levels of meaning and, therefore, new potentials for shocking spectators into a more alert level of awareness.

Naive Art

Though Naive painting has existed throughout history, the modern age has developed an especially strong appreciation for this unique approach to art. The main feature of the Naive artist's work is its unschooled self-taught character. Because the images formed by the Naive painter are made with great spontaneity, they tend to be completely free of either slickness or pretense.

Enjoying relative isolation from the formal world of art schools and commercial outlets, the Naive painter is able to preserve an unspoiled creative vision that generally takes shape in a natural sense of design. There is hardly a place on earth where Naive artists are not now working quietly, at their own pace, mostly for their own pleasure.

Cool Realism

Logically, it would seem as though the invention of the camera and the development of television should have put literal realism completely out of bounds for the creative modern painter. However, this has not happened. Evidently, there are certain elusive particulars about the look and feel of people and things that cannot be adequately treated with a camera lens. Brushes dipped in paint and stroked across a surface can still express feelings and ideas in a way that neither electronic media nor photography have been able to match.

As a veteran of World War I, Pippin painted memories from his overseas tour of duty. Once you start looking, it's hard to stop—one area leads to another in almost endless succession. Horace Pippin. *The End of the War: Starting Home*. Oil on canvas; about 1931. Collection of the Philadelphia Museum of Art.

The painted canvas of the Cool Realist is like a printout made from a computer located midway between the artist's eyeball and brain. The resulting pictures are extraordinary because they appear to be mechanically impersonal and yet, simultaneously, they are as sensitively personal as an expressive vision can be. Perhaps the key to understanding this apparent contradiction is the fact that the Cool Realists are actually very much in touch with pictures made photographically with film and electronically on television. In some mysterious way, they have internalized and humanized the methods of mechanical illustration that surround all people living today in technologically sophisticated societies.

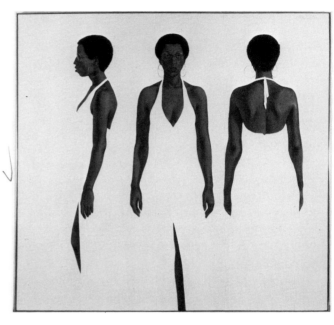

84 The left profile, full front, and rear of one person are all seen simultaneously even though that would be impossible in the *real* world. And yet, could anybody look more real than the figure in this picture? Barkley Hendricks. *October's Gone, Goodnight.* Oil and acrylic on canvas; 1973. (Photograph courtesy of the artist)

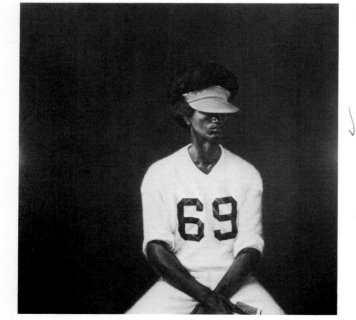

85 The subject here is oddly puzzling. While he seems almost close enough to touch, he is also far away as in some distant dream. Seated, supposedly relaxed, he could just as well spring up from the unmoving stillness that surrounds him. Barkley Hendricks. *Sammy from Miami.* Oil and acrylic on canvas; 1972. (Photograph courtesy of the artist)

Conclusion

Regardless of what directions they choose to follow, all deeply committed modern painters share certain basic motivations with each other. First and foremost, they seek to be true to their individual needs for working in art, refusing to compromise their convictions in any way whatsoever. Second, they aspire toward shaping a vocabulary of form that is distinctly their own. Finally, like the artists who have preceded them throughout history, they seek to share their language of vision with an interested and appreciative audience. For people wise enough to take advantage of their creative generosity, there is no end of enrichment to be experienced.

ACTIVITIES TO EXPLORE:

1. Make a collection of assorted materials, each having a distinctive texture of its own. Study what you have and then compose a collage design made from the odds and ends you gathered. Ask yourself the following questions. Is the design well-unified, balanced, and visually exciting to look at? Do the various parts of the total composition harmonize with each other? Are there sufficient contrasts of color, shape, and texture so that the design is not monotonous to look at?

2. With a group of friends, talk about some recent dreams you've had. If you were a Surrealist painter, what elements from these dreams would be suitable to include in a picture? Why do you think you have the dreams you have? Do your friends have dreams like yours or different from yours?

3. Are there areas of social injustice you would want to deal with in some form of artwork? Pull your ideas together in a montage-painting by combining pictures you cut out of newspapers or magazines with tempera colors you apply with a brush. Do you think such a composite form can make a more emphatic statement than either photography or paint alone?

4. Compose a pure nonrepresentational design in crayon or chalk as you listen to a passage of music on a record or on the radio. See if you can capture the mood and rhythms of the music in what you put down on the paper before you.

5. Consider possible reasons why the art of the twentieth century often looks so different from the art of the past. What facts of life in the present day may be responsible for the variety of styles we find in the contemporary art scene?

6. Do you think the invention of photography has made any difference to painters? Has the camera hindered or helped the modern artist? How? Discuss your answers to these questions with people in your class.

104

Fresh Snow on Beech Street, Moorestown N. J.

An image of a cold day on a quiet street gradually materializes in Eisenstat's pencil strokes. The lines are filled with action, darting in and out, up and down, back and forth across the entire sheet. Ben Eisenstat. *Beech Street, Moorestown*. Pencil on paper. (Photograph courtesy of the artist)

Drawings are as much a part of everyday life as speech. Even if we have no special art talent, we often find ourselves drawing simple sketches to show someone else what we want them to know. For example, we draw a quick little picture to help explain how some gadget works, to show a person how to find a street in our city, or to point out where we want a new piece of furniture placed in our home. Probably at one time or another, we have all made doodle drawings with pencil on paper while we talk to someone on the telephone.

Naturally, there is quite a difference between these ordinary everyday doodlings and diagrams and the expressive designs drawn by artists. More than random lines left by a tool haphazardly scratching over a surface, they have a life of their own, rich with emotional depth because of what the artist puts in them.

Types of Drawings

No matter what media artists use, there are three basic categories in which their drawings may be considered. At the most basic level, artists make rough sketches. These are usually brief notes of ideas that run through the artist's head. Or they may be a way of preserving something they have seen for future reference, such as an arrangement of clouds in the sky, a figure on the run, or what-ever. Second, on a more deliberate level, artists make drawings to develop ideas intended for com-pletion later in another medium. For example, pain-ters often prepare sketches or studies from which specific elements are selected for a work they are doing in oil paints or watercolor. In similar fashion, a sculptor may project ideas on paper from which particularly promising suggestions will be done

Chapter Nine

Drawing: Visual Notation in Graphic Form

The calligraphic character of oriental brush writing provides an exquisite demonstration of refined simplicity at the service of powerful expression. Konoye Nobutada. *Tenjin*. Ink on paper; about 1609. Collection of the Dallas Museum of Fine Arts; Gift of an Anonymous Foundation. (Photograph courtesy of the Dallas Museum of Fine Arts)

more permanently as forms in space. Architects and product designers frequently do the same thing because drawing offers a convenient way of exploring ideas and evaluating them without going to the trouble and expense of constructing a great number of three-dimensional models. The third category consists of drawings that are complete and finished works. Obviously, each of these kinds of drawing has a validity of its own. No particular one is automatically better than another simply because of its nature.

A very special kind of drawing outside the mainstream of the fine arts is the cartoon which expresses social and political ideas on the editorial page of a newspaper. Some of the best-known artists in our country (such as Bill Mauldin and Herbert Block) have been staff cartoonists of the various newspapers they have served over the years. Closely related to editorial cartoons are the many drawings that are prepared for use both in advertising and in magazine, newspaper, and book illustrations where pictures help tell a story more completely and effectively than do words alone.

Drawings consisting of lines alone or lines joined with tones can express a wide range of human ideas and feelings. Such designs may convey weight and volume, imply humor, describe appearances, or take us far and wide on flights of fancy.

Every artist evolves a drawing style that is right for him or her. No single approach is best for everyone because different people have different things to say and each does so in their own way.

Perhaps more than most other art forms, drawing invites a high measure of intimacy between artist and spectator. Probably because drawing is so spontaneous, it is less likely to be pretentious and postured than other avenues of making art, such as painting or printmaking, which usually must be "finished" lest they look too raw and incomplete. By comparison, when drawings become very polished, they are apt to loose the freshness and life they have when they're not quite all done. As a matter of fact, a good drawing has a decided sense of self-sufficiency. It doesn't need additional refinement, such as filling out the lines or using a heavy paint, for the graphic statement to have visual impact on the viewer. In short, a good drawing can stand on its own, free of anything extra so far as unusual techniques or materials are concerned.

"There's An Art To Analyzing Statistics"

Drawings for political commentary reach many people every day as the editorial cartoons of newspapers. Herbert Block (Herblock). *There's an Art to Analyzing Statistics*. (Reproduction with the permission of the artist)

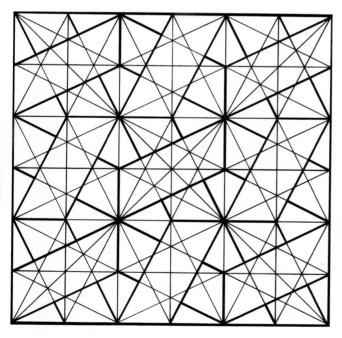

Utilizing a vocabulary and grammar of ultrapure design, Cohen's drawing generates a dynamic rather than static sense of order. Herman Cohen. *Untitled Composition*. Ink on paper. (Drawing courtesy of the artist)

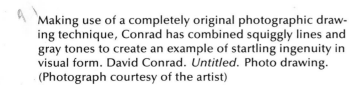

A piece of paper with inked areas drawn upon it, torn and reassembled into a new arrangement, becomes a daring and dramatic graphic statement. Jean Arp. *Composition*. Paper collage with ink wash. Philadelphia Museum of Art; A.E. Gallatin Collection.

Making use of a completely original photographic drawing technique, Conrad has combined squiggly lines and gray tones to create an example of startling ingenuity in visual form. David Conrad. *Untitled*. Photo drawing. (Photograph courtesy of the artist)

The Nature of the Image

Regardless of why artists are motivated to draw, the look and feel of their finished work is always affected by the tools they use. In the past, there were relatively few materials. The most preferred media were chalk, charcoal, and inks mixed with water and applied with pens and brushes. All these materials were inexpensive and readily available. In time, artists also used pencils, crayons, and watercolor. Now there is no limit to what artists will try in the pursuit of a graphic idea. Anything that works effectively is promptly utilized. Even scrap materials joined together in a collage have become almost commonplace. In addition, photography has opened a wide range of creative possibilities for graphic expression. So far, photography has been only slightly explored compared to accomplishments achieved with traditional drawing materials.

In the past, when people spoke of effective drawing, they usually meant an artist's ability to make literal representations in visual form. Today, the notion of quality in drawing involves more than the simple exercise of a facile hand for making representational images. After all, a camera can do that better than most people can, and from the point of view of efficiency, the camera can do the job in a fraction of a moment. Consequently, good drawing calls for the exercise of intensely human qualities that cannot be duplicated by a machine. At their best, drawings are the result of joining inventive thought and action with the artist's individual intuition and expressive drive, arriving at forms that have a distinctive visual character of their own. The most significant factor to be found in a deeply moving drawing is the artist's total commitment to a personal graphic reality. Invariably, such an image

A striking silhouette shape is fixed in place by Degas through the deft touch of chalk tones rubbed into the paper with varying degrees of pressure. The grid over the figure suggests the drawing was done as a study for a larger work which could be scaled up from the sketch, square by square. Edgar Degas. *Dancer Tying Her Sash.* Chalk on paper. The Hyde Collection; Glens Falls, New York. (Photograph by Richard K. Dean)

94 In a drawing that Leonardo may have done, the suggestion of a leafy branch is held in the figure's hand. Perhaps this was a study for his best-known painting, the *Mona Lisa*, in the collection of the Louvre Museum in Paris, France. Attributed to Leonardo da Vinci. *Mona Lisa*. Chalk on paper. The Hyde Collection; Glens Falls, New York.

93 The familiar qualities associated with Giacometti's sculpture such as slender, elongated, and isolated shapes appear in this haunting study on paper. The depth of expression is no less intense in two dimensions than it is in his more frequently seen three-dimensional work. Alberto Giacometti. *Study for Sculpture—Standing Figure*. Pencil on paper. Philadelphia Museum of Art; Louis E. Stern Collection. (Photograph by A. J. Wyatt, Staff Photographer)

is intensely original, profoundly sensitive, and richly saturated with an unmistakable emotional presence.

Whether the drawn image is firm and authoritative or delicate and hesitating, it has the potential for expressing thoughts and emotions. Your eye can follow the lines and shadows, retracing the original movements of the artist's hand. Thus, spectators can share in the process of creation, no matter how far removed from the studio by time and space.

By comparison with good work, poor drawings tend to be slick in appearance or superficial in concept. Worse yet, they may simply be stale clichés, merely mimicking the style of some popular artist rather than having an integrity of expression and an individuality of approach.

Naturally, in the final analysis, the critical evaluations we make of various graphic statements are bound to be subjective. Unless looking at art becomes a purely mechanical function, we will always differ in our judgments about any single piece of work. Therefore, opinions about art are never unanimous. Regardless of how well-informed they may seem, no art judgements can ever be absolutely objective and certain. At any rate, this is the way it has to be as long as judgments about art continue to be made by human beings and not by impersonal robotlike machines.

ACTIVITIES TO EXPLORE:

1. Make a scrapbook of the different tones and textures you can achieve with the various kinds of tools available for drawing, such as pencil, pen and ink, brush and ink, crayon, pastel chalks, and charcoal.

2. Look back to some episode you can still vividly remember from your early childhood years. Try to recapture how things looked to you then. Using crayon or chalk, make your memory come alive on a piece of paper. Put down the details as they flow through your mind. Don't hold back. Try to "let go of yourself" from inside and use simple shapes to express the images that occur to you. Work with speed and don't stop to change or correct anything. You may be quite surprised by the powerful personal statement you can put together if you really try.

3. Set up a still life (such as a book, bowl of fruit, and a vase, or other such assorted objects) on top of a table and draw what you see with at least three different drawing materials. See how the tools you use change the appearance of the pictures even though they are all interpretations of the same subject.

4. Draw a picture, in your choice of medium, of what you imagine the world and its people would look like on another planet. Feel free to let your imagination wander as far as it can.

5. Make believe you are a designer for industry. Prepare a series of drawings in which you project new directions that some familiar product might take. For example, think of automobiles and how they might look ten years from now if they were powered by a fuel other than gasoline, or develop sketches for dresses or shirts made of some disposable material which could be produced so inexpensively they would be used only one time and then discarded.

6. Take an abstract idea (such as equality, world peace, justice, or perfection) and try to express this thought in a drawing using absolutely pure (non-representational) shapes. Compare your drawing with the drawings of others in your class.

112

95 A dungeon, drawn from the depths of Piranesi's imagination, looms up vast and gloomy in an etching packed with bright highlights and dismal shadows. Giovanni Battista Piranesi. *A Prison Scene* (from the *Imaginary Prisons* series). Etching; 1760. Collection of the Philadelphia Museum of Art. (Photograph by A.J. Wyatt, Staff Photographer)

Artists make original prints in order to share creative ideas and express their feelings in a language of graphic vision. For this reason, printmaking is as significant an art activity as making a painting or a piece of sculpture.

The notion of making duplicate impressions probably goes back to the dawn of recorded history. It seems reasonable to suppose that somebody in the far distant past must have noticed that if color was applied to a raised surface and that "inked" surface was then pressed against a receptive material, an offset image or print resulted. Similarly, important people in the past used signet rings or seals to impress their special marks in a material like hot wax or damp clay which would then harden and remain stable. Such signets could be used over and over again to impress images which would duplicate each other.

History of Printmaking

Making prints on paper had to wait until someone perfected a practical printable paper. This finally happened after A.D. 100 when the Chinese developed the craft of felting vegetable fibers into paper. By the year 1000, they had so improved the product that they were able to print on a smooth, durable, and inexpensive paper surface. Using wooden blocks or smooth stones which had designs carved in them, they printed holy pictures, prayers, playing cards, and bank notes.

Printmaking came to Western Europe with the passing of the Dark Ages. At first, prints were made by stamping fabric with inked blocks of carved wood. After 1400, paper mills began to appear in various countries. Shortly after the new mills produced paper in large amounts and at reasonable cost, single-sheet woodcuts were made in quantity.

Chapter Ten

Original Graphic Prints: Multiple Impressions for People Everywhere

Artists make prints because one or another of the printmaking processes is perfectly suited to what they have to express. In this instance, etched line was the most appropriate medium Rembrandt could use for creating the atmosphere of a Dutch countryside. Rembrandt van Rijn. *The Windmill.* Etching; 1641. National Gallery of Art, Washington, D.C.; Gift of W. G. Russell Allen.

In an early example of lithography, Goya projected a terrifying moment from the world of bullfighting. With crayon strokes rubbed sensitively across the grainy surface of a printing stone, he captured all the drama and pathos of the scene. Francisco Goya. *Picador on the Horns of a Bull.* Lithograph; 1825. National Gallery of Art, Washington, D.C.; Rosenwald Collection.

The early prints pictured Christian saints and biblical scenes and were used, among other things, as playing cards and bookplates. Unfortunately, very few of these prints have survived.

The notion of original printmaking, identifying a particular artist with his print, began in Germany during the second half of the fifteenth century. At that time, various early masters began the practice of signing their initials or their name into the plates and blocks from which their printed images were made.

One of the great early masters of original printmaking, Albrecht Dürer, lived and worked in Germany during the fifteenth and early sixteenth centuries. His efforts in etching and engraving set new standards of excellence which many other artist-printmakers sought to follow.

In the seventeenth century, Rembrandt took great new strides in the art of making etchings. The black and white tones of his prints relate to the eloquent color we associate with his best paintings.

During the eighteenth century, several printmakers of first rank contributed their visions to the history of art. In England, Hogarth brought engraving in metal to an especially high peak of accomplishment. Other gifted artists of the period, which extended into the early nineteenth century, included Piranesi in Italy, Goya in Spain, and a host of talented multicolor woodcut specialists in Japan.

The range and depth of lithography were brilliantly realized during the nineteenth century by the French artist Daumier. Another Frenchman, Toulouse-Lautrec, revolutionized and vitalized multicolor printing by the lithographic process.

98 A puzzled figure from the sixteenth century ponders questions to which science, mathematics, and technology have yet to supply satisfactory answers. The composition is filled with fascinating details, from a seascape in the distance to carpentry tools in the foreground. Albrecht Dürer. *Melencolia I.* Engraving; 1514. Collection of the Philadelphia Museum of Art. (Photograph by A. J. Wyatt, Staff Photographer)

99

Multicolor woodcuts from Japan aroused enormous interest in Europe shortly after the middle of the nineteenth century. Western artists were impressed with the large areas of flat color, fluidly graceful lines, subtle treatments of pattern, and the most disciplined elimination of superfluous details. Torii Kiyonaga. *Shigeyuki Executing Calligraphy*. Multicolor woodcut; 1783. Collection of the Philadelphia Museum of Art. (Photograph by A.J. Wyatt, Staff Photographer)

The process of making prints with stencils attached to silk was known and practiced many years ago in Japan. However, it was not until the 1930s that silk-screen stencils began to be widely adopted by artists as a medium for fine printmaking. Earlier, the process had been used chiefly for commercial purposes such as printing posters and textiles.

The Nature of Printmaking

The first step in making an original print takes place when an artist develops a visual concept from which a master form or matrix is made. Often, the artist will personally prepare the matrix, as, for example, when a design is cut directly into a block of wood and then prints are made from the block. In other instances, the artist may only prepare a visual idea such as a drawing which is then translated into a printmaking matrix by an artisan who follows the artist's instructions. In this event, the artist might draw a design on the surface of a wooden block, but instead of the artist cutting it out personally, the work may be turned over to an accomplished woodcutter who actually cuts the design. Afterward, many impressions may be printed from the block. In either case, the resulting impressions are called original prints because the artist's role in creating the original form is the heart of the entire process.

While many artists do their own printing, it is not uncommon for editions to be run off by printing artisans who work closely with the artist. In either case, the artist exercises the final judgment about the quality of the finished print. Poorly printed impressions which fail to meet the artist's standards are destroyed. Generally, only satisfactory prints are kept for exhibition and sales distribution.

The buoyant spirit of a lively entertainer can still be felt today in this lithographic poster design created by Toulouse-Lautrec back in 1899. Henri Toulouse-Lautrec. *Jane Avril*. Multicolor lithograph; 1899. Collection of the Philadelphia Museum of Art.

Occasionally, only one print is made from a matrix. This may be all the artist wants. Or else, in the case of a monoprint where the matrix is a design painted on a hard smooth surface (like a piece of glass), only one print can be made since the matrix is ruined as soon as one print is pulled from the wet surface. In either of these instances, the printed impressions are called unique prints. Generally, though, artists make an edition of prints from a single matrix. Editions may vary in size anywhere from two or three impressions to several hundred impressions. In unusual instances, editions run to thousands of impressions. In either event, because they are made in editions, each print in the edition tends to be relatively inexpensive compared with one-of-a-kind objects such as oil paintings or watercolors. Furthermore, because they exist in editions, like casts of sculpture made from a master mold, original prints are often called multiple originals to distinguish them from single works of art.

Frequently, artists sign each finished print of an edition. Besides lending a personal touch to the work, the signature also authenticates the fact that each impression has met the artist's approval. Sometimes, artists also indicate the size of the edition and the serial number of a print in the edition. On the other hand, some artists refuse to limit an edition in advance. They believe as long as a matrix is in good condition and as long as it provides good prints they need not be kept from taking further impressions from the matrix.

Some artists prefer to sign their prints in the matrix rather than after the printing is done. When a signature appears in a finished print as a result of being printed from the matrix, the signature is said to be signed in the plate, signed in the stencil, signed in the stone, or signed in the block, depending upon what kind of matrix was used in making the print. However, whether a print is signed by hand, signed in the matrix, or not signed at all really makes no difference in the quality of the print as a visual object.

Even if a print is not signed, it reflects the sense of personal human involvement that went into its creation. With the exception of prints from massive editions that really are impersonal, the intimate human presence of an original print can be felt in the first as well as the last impression of a given edition. On the other hand, mechanically manufactured reproductions often lack the intangible personal essence present in an original print.

In a very real sense, original prints in multiple editions encourage art appreciation to take place on a democratic scale. Museums as well as individuals can all acquire an impression from the edition of any given print. The many impressions in an edition can therefore be thought of as a bridge where people, otherwise remote from each other in time and space, come together through their experience with the work of art shared in common by all of them.

Tooling lumber with rare skill, Newman has crafted wooden blocks from which the most unexpected of images has been given form. Libby Newman. *Ode to Jerusalem IV*. Multicolor woodcut; 1972. Benjamin Mangel Gallery, Bala-Cynwyd, Pennsylvania. (Photograph by Biagio Pinto, courtesy of the artist and the Benjamin Mangel Gallery)

The shapes, tones, and textures of Mildred Dillon's relief print reflect a personally expressive response to the sight of an old seashore hotel. Mildred Dillon. *Windsor.* Woodcut; 1959. (Photograph courtesy of the artist)

Hopper's etching is supercharged with magnetic power. The more you look, the more your eyes become attached to the bird's-eye view of brilliant light, dark shadows, and a walking figure. Edward Hopper. *Night Shadows.* Etching; 1921. IBM Art Collection. (Photograph courtesy of International Business Machines Corporation)

164 Crisp shapes constantly counterpoint each other in a composition made of shifting figure-ground oscillations and horizontal-vertical relationships. Burton Wasserman. *Eclipse.* Silk screen; 1975. Silk-screen Collection of the M. and M. Restaurant Supply Company, Division of Keystone Food Corporation, Toledo, Ohio. (Courtesy of the Benjamin Mangel Gallery, Bala-Cynwyd, Pennsylvania)

165 Almost filled to capacity with little gumballs, the glass globe mounted on its base also looks like an electric bulb screwed into a giant socket. Marilyn Ross. *Gumballs.* Multicolor intaglio print; 1973. (Photograph courtesy of the artist)

The playful shapes and varied tones of Maitin's silk screen identify an organic sense of form. Sam Maitin. *The Wharton Print*. Silk screen; 1974. (Photograph courtesy of the artist)

ACTIVITIES TO EXPLORE:

1. Go to the library and see what you can learn about some of the great printmakers of the past such as Dürer, Rembrandt, Goya, Hogarth, Daumier, and Toulouse-Lautrec. If you can get to a large metropolitan museum, you might also want to ask for examples of original works by these artists which the museum is likely to have in their permanent collection.

2. By checking into books specifically concerned with original graphic prints, see if you can learn about the differences that exist between the four traditional methods of printmaking: relief, intaglio, lithography, and stenciling.

3. Try your hand at making some original prints using a piece of linoleum as the material for the matrix. You can learn excactly what to do by asking your art teacher what steps are involved in the process.

4. After you've made some prints from linoleum, try to see if you can also make a print from a block of wood. The same tools you used for cutting the linoleum will work fine with wood.

5. As a change of pace from block printing, you may enjoy making a silk-screen print. The necessary materials are relatively inexpensive. If you need help in getting everything together, talk to your art teacher about how to proceed. You can also find books in a library that show and tell exactly what to do.

Beyond the representation of a ferocious jungle cat, the artist has also provided a visual catalog of the many different tones and textures that can be cut into a block of wood. Misch Kohn. *Tiger.* Wood engraving. Collection of the Philadelphia Museum of Art.

Though creative people have been involved with printmaking for a long time, patrons of the arts have not always valued prints for their originality. As a matter of fact, until the end of the nineteenth century, the procedures used for printmaking were put to work chiefly for the purpose of preparing and marketing inexpensive copies of famous paintings and drawings. However, with the arrival of good photoengraving in the twentieth century, it soon became obvious that handmade reproductive printmaking was generally inferior to photo-mechanical reproduction, insofar as reproductive fidelity and economy of costs were concerned. And so, little by little, the handmade reproductive print has faded from favor. At the same time, increasing attention has been given to the notion of the artist as a unique and sensitive individual with something personal to express in a language of graphic form.

Chapter Eleven

Modern Developments in Creative Printmaking

The New Outlook

More creative printmaking has emerged in the twentieth century than in all the preceding years of the past. As artists explored the possibilities at their disposal for making original prints, their work took on the look and feel of one or more of the movements that have surfaced in the contemporary period. The same trends and developments that have taken place in the field of painting have had a parallel development in printmaking. As a consequence, original prints have appeared which bear the flavor and stamp of such diverse schools as Expressionism, Fauvism, Surrealism, and so on.

As a rule, artists who follow the Expressionist tradition deal with figurative subject matter. Most frequently, people, places, and things take shape in

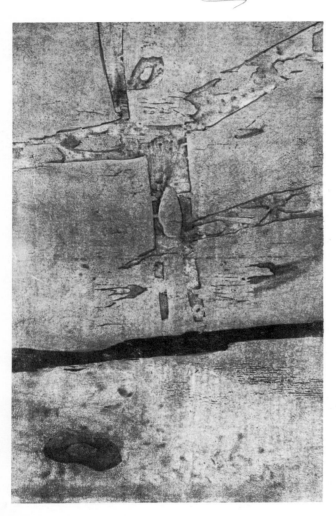

Based upon an ancient mythological story, Newman's abstract impression of the subject has been rendered with great care and sensitive control. Libby Newman. *Daedalus and Icarus*. Multicolor woodcut. (Photograph courtesy of the artist and the Benjamin Mangel Gallery, Bala-Cynwyd, Pennsylvania)

their compositions. On occasion, they bring a lyrical touch to what they've seen. At other times, they turn a critical eye upon their surroundings or upon the contemporary state of the human condition. What they have to say then often speaks in a harsh and vigorous idiom of graphic expression.

A second major source of creative form and expression grew out of Cubism. In a very general way, this approach may be referred to as Abstraction.

Yet another approach has evolved in which artists eliminate all reference to the object world. Instead of making a pictorial image, they explore a wide range of intuitively felt ideas generated within their imagination. They create universes of pure color and texture. Through their work, they take invisible realities felt within themselves and make them visible as form.

Recent Trends

The search to expand ways and means available for making prints has had a profound effect on how prints look. For example, until quite recently, prints were usually small in scale. Generally, the number of colors used for a given image was quite limited. By comparison, today it is not unusual to see huge prints, two feet by three feet in area and even larger with a seemingly unlimited range of colors and color combinations.

New ways of shaping form continue to be advanced by artists at the frontiers of today's art community. Typically, certain printmakers freely mix different processes in order to create new kinds of visual images. Still others make use of modern industrial technology such as process cameras and offset lithopresses. Clearly, much of

Appelson's woodcut makes bold use of crisp-edged shapes. The face of the subject touches your eye with potent optical energy and a deeply moving human consciousness. Herbert Appelson. *Butcher Shop*. Woodcut. (Photograph courtesy of the artist)

Conceived with formalistic precision, Marcoussis's Cubist abstraction is a good example of dignified balance and measured control. Louis Marcoussis. *Portrait of Guillaume Apollinaire*. Drypoint. Philadelphia Museum of Art; Louise and Walter Arensberg Collection. (Photograph by A.J. Wyatt, Staff Photographer)

As a rule, Lebrun's print of a figure on crutches evokes a compassionate human response from spectators. Rico Lebrun. *The Rabbit*. Lithograph. IBM Art Collection. (Photograph courtesy of International Business Machines Corporation)

112 Moving in toward the center and then drifting out to the edges, the design generates a rhythm approximating the breath of life. The perfect flowerlike symmetry is similar to the balanced forms that often appear in nature. Richard Hood. *Symmetry in Bloom.* Silk screen. (Photograph courtesy of the artist)

113 Lichtenstein's print explodes with a wild combination of comic strip violence and sober compositional control. Roy Lichtenstein. *Crak Poster.* Offset lithograph. Collection of the Philadelphia Museum of Art. (Photograph by A. J. Wyatt, Staff Photographer)

the image content in their work grows out of the unusual equipment they use.

In some cases, such high relief surfaces are achieved in paper that the resulting print is not just sculpturesque it is actually a piece of relief sculpture. Also, there are prints so deeply embossed, in some instances without ink, that each print looks and feels like a reverse bas-relief sculpture.

Recently, very imaginative procedures for making prints from both raised and lowered portions of a plate have resulted in impressions called collographs. To make a collograph matrix, various materials are attached to a base. As in the case of intaglio printmaking, it is possible to apply ink on different levels of the plate in one or more colors and then have them all print on the paper at one time.

Other new techniques that artists are currently exploring include perforating their prints, using industrial inks, and printing on either flat or multisurface pieces of plastic, cloth, rubber, and metal. Until recently, none of these practices were carried out in a printmaker's workshop. Without doubt, some of these novel adventures into the unfamiliar will produce little of lasting merit. On the other hand, it is quite possible that very significant achievements will emerge.

While printmaking processes are all different, no single one is completely perfect. Each has distinct advantages and disadvantages. Whether artists use one process or another is not as important as how well they use the process they have chosen to translate a particular graphic idea into a finished print.

Various circular elements attached to a base and coated with different colors of ink were used to make this collograph print. The repeating shapes have a hypnotic icon-like effect that grows in power the longer you look at it. Seena Donneson. *Mandala X.* Collograph. (Photograph by O. E. Nelson, courtesy of the artist)

ACTIVITIES TO EXPLORE:

1. Visit an art gallery where modern original prints are exhibited and carefully examine the variety of styles in which different artists work. Do the variations of style say something about the individual differences that exist between one artist and another?

2. If someone wanted to give you a work of art as a gift and offered you a choice between an inexpensive original print that appealed to you and a high-priced one-of-a-kind oil painting you didn't particularly care for, which one would you take? Why?

3. Compare the pictures of modern prints and modern paintings reproduced in this book. Can you find stylistic parallels between any of them?

4. Do you think printmaking has anything in common with making drawings? Why?

5. Go to the library and see what you can find out about great modern painters who have also distinguished themselves as printmakers. (Here is a little hint to help you in your explorations: check on the creative developments of Pablo Picasso, Marc Chagall, and Joan Miró.)

6. Select a simple printmaking technique (such as potato printing or the silk-screen process) for preparing a small edition of impressions you can then use as a seasonal greeting card. Would people you care about enjoy receiving something so distinctly personal from you?

Exploring new ways of creating prints, Naomi Limont has evolved a mystical vocabulary of personal expression. Deep embossing and delicately fanciful shapes join each other in a lyrical language of form. Naomi Limont. *Grassy Kolle*. Combination graphic. (Photograph by Alexander Limont, courtesy of the artist)

To make this inkless, embossed design, dedicated to the late President John F. Kennedy, Margo first dissolved celluloid (plastic) in a solvent. The resulting liquid was then brushed onto the printing plate with considerable fluidity and flexibility of execution. Boris Margo. *In Memoriam.* Cellocut. IBM Collection. (Photograph courtesy of International Business Machines)

117 The huge (60 feet high) images were created for the sake of rendering tribute to Rameses's greatness as a warrior-king. *Rameses II*. Abu Simbel Temple. 1257 B.C. (Photograph by Solshi Afifi, courtesy of the Egyptian Government Ministry of Tourism)

118 Carved by an unknown prehistoric artist, the tiny sculpture (4⅜ inches high) is surprisingly monumental in the breadth and scale of its concept. The vitality of the bulging figure suggests a goddess of nature, devoted to abundant human fertility and nourishment. *Venus of Willendorf*. Limestone carving; created between 30,000 and 10,000 B.C. Collection of the Museum of Natural History, Vienna, Austria.

Sculptors work with form in space. Using three-dimensional materials, they organize solid masses and open volumes. Sometimes they make tiny statuettes and, at other times, monumental works of enormous size. But whatever the scale or the material they use, they seek to invest what they make with an intensity and depth of feeling.

Early Origins

The oldest piece of carved stone in existence today, called the *Venus of Willendorf,* was found in Austria. It was probably made during the Stone Age to express the importance of human fertility. The exaggerated anatomy of the figure suggests the work was a representation of some maternity goddess. As such, the sculpture probably had great significance as a religious object, symbolizing the ability of a deity to provide people on earth with the gift of life.

In ancient times, sculpture was also used to express the great power held by political officials such as Egyptian pharaohs and the governors of city states situated in the Mesopotamian Valley (a region in the Middle East between the Tigris and Euphrates rivers). Typically, the mighty sculptures of *Ramses II* from the old Abu Simbel Temple on the Nile River represent a semidivine personage presiding over his subjects with rights vested in him by a higher authority. The statue *Gudea,* carved in a black stone called diorite, is a representation of a priest-king who ruled Lagash, a long-extinct Mesopotamian municipality.

Closer to home, we find much early sculpture in Mexico, which was a civilized country long before the arrival of explorers from Spain in the sixteenth

Chapter Twelve

Sculpture: Expressive Art in Three Dimensions

century. Pre-Columbian Mexican sculpture, in particular, is strangely fascinating. The rigidity of the forms expresses an awesome dignity, quiet refinement, and balanced strength.

The Great Traditions

Throughout history, sculptors have dealt with common themes that tie all peoples together. Typically, the desire to memorialize heroic individuals, express beauty, or illuminate religious principles appears again and again.

The ancient Greeks created sculpture reflecting their belief in the importance of harmony and order in every aspect of life. The exquisite nature of their forms expresses their unique philosophical outlook. To the Greeks, the physical, intellectual, and emotional sides of human makeup were expected to be brought into accord with each other and regulated with an almost perfect state of balance. A superb example of this viewpoint is provided by the *Discus Thrower.* In much the same fashion, a tenth-century bronze *Buddha* from Cambodia expresses a feeling of great dignity and peaceful composure.

A complex sequence of strenuous movements has been transformed by the sculptor into a single gracefully balanced image in three dimensions. Myron. *Discobolus* (Discus Thrower). Roman copy in marble, based upon a bronze original of about 450 B.C. Collection of the Vatican Museum, Rome, Italy. (Photograph by S. D. Anderson, courtesy of Alinari)

Mexican sculpture from the pre-Columbian period differs considerably in appearance from European art of the same period. Nevertheless, the forms have been rendered with great sensitivity and a profound sense of humanity. *Seated Man and Woman.* Ceramicware from Jalisco, Mexico; approximately 100 B.C. Collection of the Dallas Museum of Fine Arts; purchased with a gift from Mr. and Mrs. Eugene McDermott and the McDermott Foundation and Mr. and Mrs. Algur H. Meadows and the Meadows Foundation, Incorporated. (Photograph courtesy of the Dallas Museum of Fine Arts)

Quiet composure and regal authority are readily identified in this awesome seated figure. *Buddha Enthroned.* Bronze from Cambodia; nineteenth century. Collection of the Kimbell Museum, Fort Worth, Texas. (Photograph by Bob Wharton, courtesy of the Kimbell Museum)

The smooth flow of rounded contours, restrained elegance, and reserved dignity all complement each other in this compact sculpture from ancient Mesopotamia. An interesting added touch is the statement in cuneiform letters spelled out on the drapery wrapped around the legs of the seated figure. *Gudea.* Diorite carving; approximately 2050 B.C. (Photograph courtesy of the University Museum, University of Pennsylvania, Philadelphia, Pennsylvania)

In classic Roman sculpture, we usually find memorials of various emperors and other important people, carved in marble. Because the Romans were especially fond of realistic portraiture, they evolved a highly representational approach to form. As the other illustration here (of George Washington) shows, the creation of memorial tributes in sculpture have continued to be a major tradition in Western art.

In the fourth century, the Roman Empire accepted Christianity as the official religion of the state. Ever since then, artists have worked in behalf of the Church and its precepts. Needless to say, other societies all over the world have also used the talents of creative people for the sake of expressing their own particular spiritual beliefs.

Seated erectly, the stately gesture and commanding pose of the figure express the dignity and authority of the nation's first president. Horatio Greenough. *George Washington.* Marble; height, 11 feet 4 inches; 1832–1840. National Collection of Fine Arts, Smithsonian Institution, Washington, D.C.

The stone portrait of Vespasian, a Roman emperor of the first century, is very realistic and unpretentious. *Head of Vespasian.* Marble; about A.D. 75. Collection of the National Museum of Rome, Italy. (Photograph courtesy of Alinari)

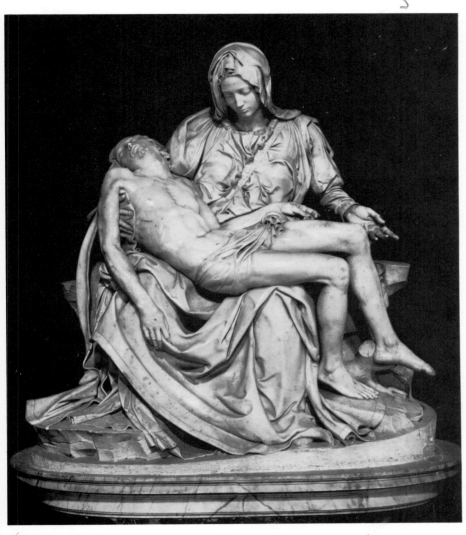

An intensity of religious devotion is clearly evident in Michelangelo's *Pieta*. Michelangelo Buonarroti. *Pieta*. Marble; height 69 inches; 1501. Basilica of Saint Peter's, Rome, Italy. (Photograph by S. D. Anderson, courtesy of Alinari)

This carving has a symbolic character, embodying the sense of a spirit rather than being a representational form. As a sacred object, the sculpture was believed to be endowed with great religious power. *Wooden Figure of a Man*. Ivory Coast; Baoulé. Early twentieth century. (Photograph courtesy of the University Museum, University of Pennsylvania, Philadelphia, Pennsylvania)

For thousands of years, sculpture has been used in connection with architecture. The example provided here from the Cathedral of Notre Dame in Chartres, France, had considerable relevance to the age in which it was made. The monumental construction by Gabo was developed for placement beside the clean-cut Bijenkorf department store of Rotterdam in the Netherlands. The heroic *Head of a Woman* by Picasso occupies a place of distinction specifically planned for it by the architects of the Municipal Civic Center in the city of Chicago.

As all these examples show, there is no single approach to creating art that is absolutely superior to all others. Every culture and every period of time is a complex composite with a distinctive makeup of its own. This fact explains why forms produced by artists living in different cultures and during different epochs in history should not be expected to look alike, even if the underlying reasons for making them have much in common with each other across time and space.

Sculptors can turn to a wide variety of materials when they are ready to proceed with a piece of work. This initial choice is critical because it affects how the artist will structure forms in space.

Great dignity is evident in these stone carvings from the Gothic period. Column statues at the Cathedral of Notre Dame de Chartres. Chartres, France. 1145–1170. (Photograph courtesy of the Services Culturels de l'Ambassade de France, New York, New York)

Open space becomes an exciting tangible element in this construction of Naum Gabo. Brilliantly engineered, this is the largest piece of work (80 feet high) using a purely Constructivist orientation to be found anywhere in the world. Naum Gabo. *Rotterdam Construction*. 1957. Bijenkorf Store, Rotterdam, The Netherlands. (Photograph by Tom Kroeze, courtesy of Bijenkorf Store, Rotterdam)

Picasso's abstraction of a human head is a fascinating study in open volume and flat planes. The physical features (eyes, nose, nostrils, lips, chin, and hair) counterpoint the transparent reality of air flowing freely through the steel rods and plates. Pablo Picasso. *Head of a Woman*. Steel. 1965. Chicago Civic Center. (Photograph by Bob Murphy, courtesy of the city of Chicago, Department of Development and Planning)

Carving

By using hard materials such as stone or wood, sculptors eliminate all unnecessary material until they're left with the finished piece. Therefore, in carving, it is just as important to know when to stop as it is to know where to cut away waste matter.

Because most carving materials are quite resistant to the action of hand tools, they offer a challenge many sculptors find deeply stimulating and exciting. However, the very fact of their resistance makes it essential for the artist to have a well-defined idea of what the shape of a finished work will be. Spontaneous improvisation cannot be impulsively exercised in carving.

Of course, the material selected contributes a great deal to the eventual expressiveness of a finished piece. Therefore, the color of a particular kind of stone, its durability, and its internal structure all need to be taken into account in the overall design of a projected sculptural idea.

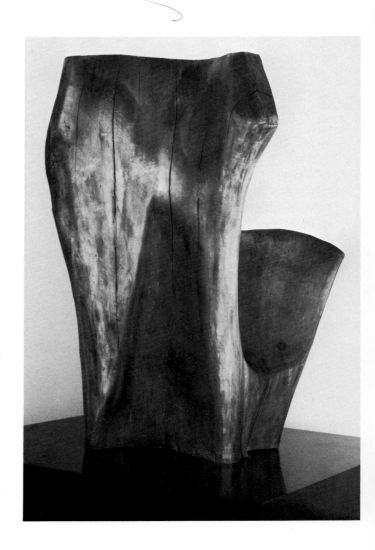

The shapes carved in wood carry on a dialogue with the space flowing about and between them. Raoul Hague. *Groeg Kill*. Carved wood; 1970. (Photograph by John A. Ferrari, courtesy of the Zabriskie Gallery, New York, New York)

In dealing with wood, one of the most intriguing aspects of the material, besides a wide range of possible colors, is its fibrous and grainy nature. Taking note of these basic facts about the makeup of the medium and incorporating them into the design of any particular piece of work adds considerable to the integrity, appearance, and expressiveness of the finished piece. Obviously, if the structure of the grain in the block of lumber is inconsistent with a particular sculptural concept, the sculptor would be better off discarding that chunk of wood in favor of another whose grain characteristics are appropriate.

While most carving is done in stone and wood, sculptors also occasionally use such materials as ivory and plaster. Clearly, the materials used for carving are relatively stable and therefore capable of retaining the shapes tooled into them.

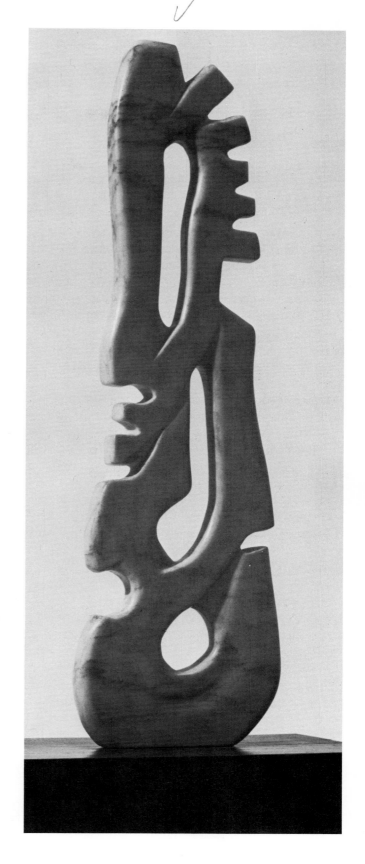

With endless internal energy, intertwining forms reach a zenith and turn about downward again. Bernard Petlock. *As a Watch in the Night.* Carved marble. 1972. (Photograph by John H. Busser, Jr., courtesy of the artist)

Modeling

By contrast with carving, a subtractive process in which waste material is gradually removed until the final form is revealed, modeling is an additive approach. Lumps of pliable material are added to each other with thoughtful care and constant refinement until the piece is completed. The most commonly used modeling media are clay and wax. Because they are quite soft and have little tensile strength, modeling materials are generally built up on armatures made of wood or metal.

One of the oldest modeling materials in the world, terra-cotta, is still used today. Terra-cotta is clay that has been dug from the ground, shaped into some specific form, and then fired (baked hard in a kiln or oven) at a high temperature. Sometimes, the finished piece is coated with paint. Another procedure for lending greater permanence and beauty to clay consists of adding various color effects to the work, followed by an application of glaze and refiring at a higher temperature in the kiln. Pieces thus decorated and glazed are often more appealing than plain bisque, that is, terra-cotta fired without glaze.

A modeled form may be made even more permanent by having a mold made and then casting a very durable material such as bronze, other metals, concrete, plaster, or plastic in the mold. In addition to greater strength and a wider range of possible visual effects, castings made in sturdy materials can be duplicated over and over again as long as there is a desire for them and as long as the molds remain in satisfactory working condition.

The touch of the artist's fingers can still be felt in the surface appearance of the baked clay. The modeled forms were further intensified by the application of a paint in different colors to lend greater naturalness to the sculpture. Andrea del Verrocchio. *Lorenzo de Medici.* Modeled terra-cotta, painted. c. 1485. National Gallery of Art, Washington, D.C.; Samuel H. Kress Collection.

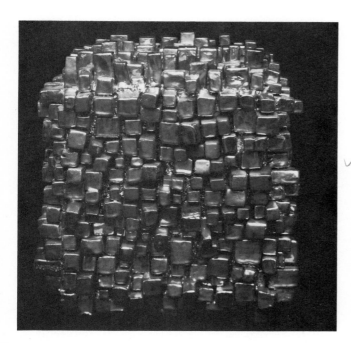

33 More than a hundred different tones of silver ripple across the surface of the glazed ceramic sculpture. The contrast between the earthy solidity of the fired clay and the airy brightness of the reflected light contributes additional levels of visual meaning to the work. John Costanza. Ceramic sculpture with silver lustre glaze. 1972. (Photograph courtesy of the artist)

34 A sense of profound intensity can be felt in the exploded spherical forms in bronze by Arnaldo Pomodoro. Arnaldo Pomodoro. *Sphere Number Six*. Bronze; 1963–1965. Hirshhorn Museum and Sculpture Garden, Smithsonian Institution, Washington, D.C.

142

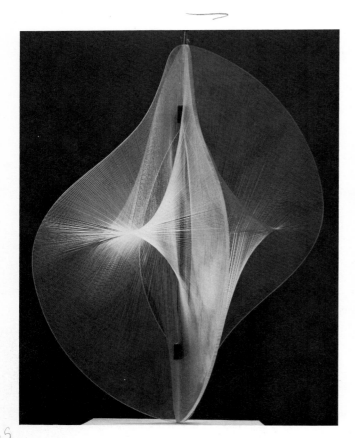

The effortless grace of the Gabo construction almost dissolves the force of gravity, leaving the forms free to float forever in an endless sea of space. Naum Gabo. *Linear Construction Number Two.* Construction; acrylic plastic and nylon thread; 1949. Collection of the Stedilijk Museum, Amsterdam, The Netherlands. (Photograph courtesy of the Stedelijk Museum)

Differences between the curved and rectilinear shapes are taken a step further in the contrast of the open and closed areas of constructed form. Louise Nevelson. *Atmosphere and Environment.* Construction; bolted and welded sections of Corten steel. 1970. Putnam Memorial Collection; Princeton University, Princeton, New Jersey. (Photograph by Marie E. Bellis, courtesy of Princeton University)

Constructing

When three-dimensional media are joined together with paste, nails, screws, rivets, or by welding and bolting, the resulting forms have a constructed or assembled look, quite different from either carving or modeling.

Construction offers sculptors a vast range of new opportunities for exploring space relationships with elements that stand still or move. In addition, some modern artists have also been exploring new ways of dealing with electric power and light in their constructed forms.

Obviously, there is no limit to the materials sculptors can use in making constructions. So far, metals, wood, string, wire, cloth, cardboard, paper, and every sort of synthetic plastic have been put to work in the creation of unusual and daring ventures in space and form.

A pointed commentary on life, touched with a note of whimsy, emerges from Entwisle's constructed composition. William Entwisle. *Treadmill.* Construction; found objects and polyester resin built directly on armatures. 1964. (Photograph courtesy of the artist)

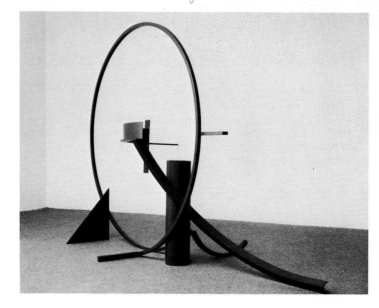

Todd's welded construction is a piece of free-standing sculpture in which open space and transparent shapes are as important to the total experience of the forms as the materials used to assemble the work. Mike Todd. *Sengai Circle II.* Welded steel; 1972. (Photograph by John A. Ferrari, courtesy of the Zabriskie Gallery, New York, New York)

Figures of this type were fastened to reliquary baskets in which treasured bones of revered ancestors were placed and kept in family shrines by the Bakota people of Africa. *Funerary Figures*. From the Congo. Construction; strips of copper and brass overlaid on wood. Early twentieth century. (Photograph courtesy of The University Museum, University of Pennsylvania, Philadelphia, Pennsylvania)

Forms in Relief and in the Round

Besides the materials and processes used in structuring pieces of work, sculptors must also decide whether their forms will exist in relief or in the round.

Works that may be seen from all sides, revealing their total configuration as spectators move about and see them in their entirety, are referred to as sculpture in the round. When they are situated on the floor or upon a pedestal they are also called free-standing pieces. On the other hand, a relief is a sculpture in which parts of the work stand forth from a solid background. When the projections come forward relatively low from the back-base, the work is called bas-relief (pronounced "bah," the "s" is silent). The word "bas" comes from the French word for low. In addition, it is also possible to find medium-relief and high-relief work.

Sculptors are deeply concerned not only with techniques but also with what they have to say. Clearly, technical competence alone does not make great art. Selecting and shaping materials are only means to the artists' ultimate end: creating a language of form capable of expressing their innermost feelings and thoughts with conviction and creative sensitivity.

This work by Jean Arp in which irregularly shaped elements appear against a flat background base provides a good illustration of a bas-relief sculpture. Jean Arp. *Constellation*. Painted wood relief; 1932. Philadelphia Museum of Art; Louise and Walter Arensberg Collection. (Photograph courtesy of the Philadelphia Museum of Art)

While the horizontal and vertical members of this example protrude but slightly from the background, the third element, spatially perpendicular to the base, is obviously in high relief within the total form of the construction. Burton Wasserman. *1966-CA*. Painted wood relief; 1966.

ACTIVITIES TO EXPLORE

1. Visit a museum and seek out the three-dimensional pieces in their collection. Compare the different media and structuring techniques that were used to create the work on view.

2. Choose a subject which interests you for modeling in clay. Make something with which you're familiar such as a pet dog or cat, or perhaps a horse or a snake.

3. Arrange a group of wooden scraps and pieces of metal into an interesting three-dimensional composition. With an appropriate adhesive, you should be able to join various parts together with no difficulty whatsoever.

4. Make a bas-relief carving in a flat slab of damp (leather hard) clay. Whittle into the material carefully so that a three-dimensional form gradually stands out from a solid background. For your first try, you might want to use relatively simple geometric shapes as the basis of your design.

5. Get some inexpensive iron wire which can be easily shaped by hand or with a small pair of pliers. First, practice bending and twisting the wire to develop familiarity with the material. When you feel you have control over it, see if you can represent a human figure or create a comical caricature with the wire.

6. Compare the expressiveness of sculpture from different cultures and different periods of time. What makes them unlike each other in appearance? In what ways are they similar? Why?

The surface of Rodin's sculpture reflects light with considerable richness and depth. In heroic proportions, the
modeled forms express the capacity all people have for
deep thought. Auguste Rodin. *The Thinker.* Bronze;
1879–1889. National Gallery of Art, Washington, D.C.;
Gift of Mrs. John W. Simpson.

The nineteenth century provided the right time and place for new breakthroughs in sculpture. More than any other single person, Auguste Rodin proved to be the bridge between the past and the present. Stated briefly, Rodin did for sculpture what the Impressionists and Post-Impressionits did for painting.

Like the Impressionists, Rodin studied how light and atmosphere reveal a subject. Though he made some carvings, Rodin favored clay which can be cast in a hard and permanent substance like bronze after the modeling has been completed. Dealing with such a highly plastic medium, he could manipulate subtle nuances in a surface with his fingers just as a painter might pat a paint-tipped brush in deft strokes across a canvas. However, though Rodin's treatment of flickering light lends an Impressionistic identity to his work, he also managed to impart a distinctive sense of monumental grandeur and dramatic gesture to his work.

Early Beginnings

Perhaps more than anyone else, the one artist who stands out as the great pioneer of modern sculpture in the twentieth century is Constantin Brancusi. It is almost impossible to see his work and not be affected emotionally. Some people seeing his art for the first time have been moved to tears. Others find an irresistible impulse rising within them to touch the surfaces of his pieces in stone, wood, or bronze because they have such a tactile richness.

Following in the footsteps of Brancusi, Henry More and Jean Arp explored the nature of biomorphic shapes as a foundation for expressive form. With extraordinary eloquence, they have created

Chapter Thirteen

Focus on Modern Sculpture

deeply moving organic presences in their carvings, castings, and reliefs.

Working in absolutely pure nonrepresentational form, Naum Gabo has created striking metaphors projecting idealized realities of constructive thought and feeling. With great precision, his forms suggest how much more worthwhile it is to build rather than destroy.

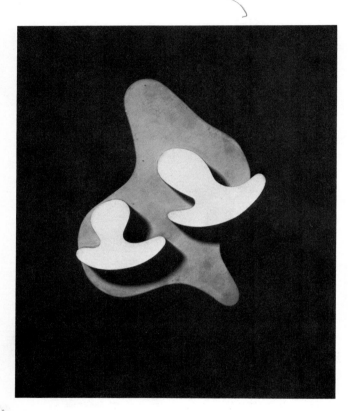

143 All the curvilinear shapes in Arp's composition add up to a richly rhythmic unity expressed in organic terms. Jean Arp. *Vase-Bust*. Painted wood relief; 1930. Philadelphia Museum of Art; A.E. Gallatin Collection. (Photograph courtesy of the Philadelphia Museum of Art)

144 The strength and character of a stone block have been successfully preserved in Brancusi's abstract carving of two people kissing each other with gentle tenderness. Constantin Brancusi. *The Kiss*. Carved stone; 1908. Philadelphia Museum of Art; Louise and Walter Arensberg Collection. (Photograph courtesy of the Philadelphia Museum of Art)

145 The design of Moore's sculpture consists of rounded surfaces melting into each other with a mysteriously silent sense of order and subtle grace. Henry Moore. *Oval with Points*. Bronze, 11 feet high; 1969. Putnam Memorial Collection; Princeton University. (Photograph by Marie Bellis, courtesy of Princeton University)

146 With the insight of an engineer's feeling for tension and resolution, Gabo has harmoniously combined a solid stone mass with a series of open volumes defined by the crisp edges of planes curved in space. Naum Gabo. *Stone with a Collar*. Construction, Portland stone, slate base, and Perspex plastic; 1933. (Photograph courtesy of the artist)

The Humanist Tradition

While abstraction became an important new direction in twentieth-century sculpture, many artists continued to explore representational forms, especially the human figure, for the sake of expressing their insights. However, there was no uniform approach. Aristide Maillol went back to the ancient Greek ideas of sculpturesque form. To the classic pose he brought a smoothly flowing sense of form rooted in earthy solidity. By contrast, the carvings of Amadeo Modigliani are strangely spiritual with masklike faces inspired by the study of African art. His work reflects the sculpture of far-flung primitive peoples as well as the simplifications of form found in Cubist painting.

Any discussion of modern figurative art would surely be incomplete without reference to Pablo Picasso. Probably no other creative personality has done as much to express the human spirit in as many different dimensions and as imaginatively as he did during his lifetime. Certainly, nobody has expressed a sense of the monumental as convincingly in any form as he did in the great heads he designed in steel (see chapter 12) and poured concrete.

What Picasso dealt with in grandeur, Alberto Giacometti treated with slender details that are so hauntingly mysterious you find yourself wondering if they really exist at all. His tootpick-thin creatures skirt a fine line between being and nothingness, expressing areas of feeling experienced at one time or other by every person alive.

Combining poetic melancholy, free distortion, and the influence of African art forms, Modigliani achieved the expression of an intensely aloof solitude and nobility. Amadeo Modigliani. *Head of a Woman*. Carved limestone; c. 1910. National Gallery of Art, Washington, D.C.; Chester Dale Collection.

Constantly thinning his forms to reach their ultimate essence, Giacometti arrived at figures treading a fine line between existence and sheer nothingness. Alberto Giacometti. *Place*. Bronze; 1948–1949. Collection of the Emanuel Hoffman Foundation; Kunstmuseum Basel. (Photograph courtesy of the Emanuel Hoffman Foundation and the Kunstmuseum Basel)

Fifteen feet high and weighing ten tons, Picasso's sculpture in poured concrete projects a most formidable presence. Pablo Picasso. *Head of a Woman.* Poured concrete; 1962. Putnam Memorial Collection, Princeton University. (Photograph courtesy of Princeton University)

With deep admiration for the sculpture of ancient Greece, Maillol sought to express serene poise and measured order. Aristide Maillol. *Venus.* Bronze; 1918–1928. National Gallery of Art, Washington, D.C.; Ailsa Mellon Bruce Fund.

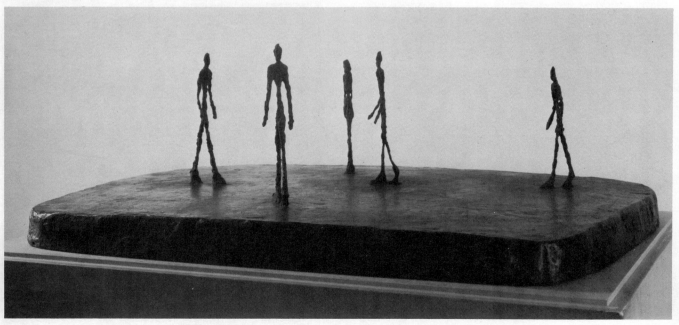

151
Responsive to the slightest shift in direction by an air current, the total structure made of flat metal fins can suddenly change its configuration as all the parts move in relation to each other. Alexander Calder. *Cascading Red.*
Hanging mobile in metal. (Photograph courtesy of Perls
Galleries, New York)

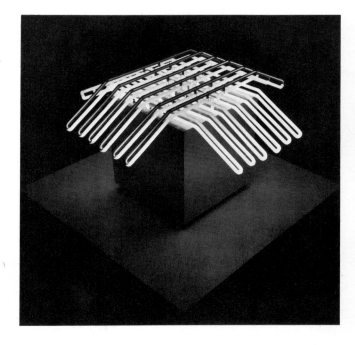

152
Hovering in space, the lines of neon light glow with an
amazingly cool reserve. Stephen Antonakos. *Ruby and
Yellow Neon.* Construction; neon light tubing and metal;
1967. (Photograph by John A. Ferrari, courtesy of the John
Weber Gallery, New York)

Kinetic Sculpture

A mobile is a composite of abstract forms sus-
pended in space. While it is virtually a household
word today, it wasn't when Alexander Calder first
began making mobiles in the 1930s. His forms are
so exquisitely balanced and soundly engineered
that they promptly respond to the most delicate
currents of wind moving through the air. His
sculpture becomes an object in motion, animated
from within its own structure and constantly changing its profile in space.

Since Calder's initial work in dealing with motion,
other artists have not only explored free movement
but also put electricity to work generating motion
in three dimensions. By the use of their creative vision, they help us see and feel how electrical energy
and other forces moving through space are significant realities, often overlooked by people even
though they are constantly in touch with them at
every turn.

Recent Developments

With each passing day, sculptors are making greater
and greater use of materials and structuring
techniques borrowed directly from the world of
technology. Typically, forms are made with rope,
steel, glass, concrete, plastics, aluminum, rubber,
neon tubing, and electrical wiring. The materials
are often joined together by such procedures as
welding, nailing, riveting, and bolting, and by using
all sorts of industrial adhesives. In many cases,
finished pieces of sculpture look as though they
might have rolled off an assembly line in a factory
somewhere instead of being put together in an artist's studio.

Stankiewicz uses the materials and structuring techniques
of modern industrial technology to excellent advantage in
the forms he fashions in three dimensions. Richard Stankiewicz. *1973–3*. Welded Steel; 1973. (Photograph by
John A. Ferrari, courtesy of the Zabriskie Gallery, New
York)

154

156 Wagner renders truth and beauty with a grammar of design stripped to the barest minimum essentials. Her forms are metaphysical voids filled with an eloquently monumental nobility. G. Noble Wagner. *Untitled*. Welded stainless steel; 1974. (Photograph courtesy of the artist and the Marion Locks Gallery, Philadelphia)

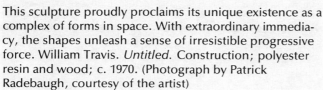

154 This sculpture proudly proclaims its unique existence as a complex of forms in space. With extraordinary immediacy, the shapes unleash a sense of irresistible progressive force. William Travis. *Untitled*. Construction; polyester resin and wood; c. 1970. (Photograph by Patrick Radebaugh, courtesy of the artist)

155 Light striking the various steel facets is reflected in a continuously changing pattern of lustre and shadow. David Smith. *Cubi XIII*. Construction; welded stainless steel; 1963. Putnam Memorial Collection, Princeton University. (Photograph by Marie Bellis, courtesy of Princeton University)

Today's sculptors employ materials they find in their environment and put them to good use in previously undreamed of ways. They have generated a wide range of images with a vividly authentic sense of the here and now. For that reason alone, much of their work is inviting. Beckoning to us with a feeling of familiarity, they reveal feelings, associations, and ideas that have a ring of contemporary truth. Thus, many modern sculptors educate our eyes to become more aware of interesting colors and textures all around us. Because we often overlook our everyday surroundings, we deprive ourselves of much that could otherwise give enrichment to our lives if only we were more sensitive to them. On the other hand, a lot of new sculpture also shows the grime and emptiness of the urban scene. The difference between this art experience and the ordinary view we have of the city and its manufacturing plants is due to the intensified feeling we experience when in contact with an art object. Outside, on a city street, all sorts of distractions prevent us from focusing attention as carefully as we do in a gallery or a museum.

More than ever before, sculptors today find themselves driven by a need to continue the never-ending search for new ways of identifying and expressing what they know and feel. Side by side with scientists seeking to learn about every-thing in the universe, artists are venturing forth into every possible kind of space in order to deepen and widen the language of vision at their command.

ACTIVITIES TO EXPLORE:

1. Is there any sculpture in public places where you live or go to school? What does the sculpture do for the area where it was placed?

2. Think about the different forms of three-dimensional art you read about in this chapter. Which ones appealed to you the most and which ones the least? Why?

3. Can you think of any setting in your community that would be enriched by the presence of some sculptures? What would work best in the location you have in mind?

4. Make some rough "sketches" with clay (in three dimensions) for sculptures you think would look good at a sports stadium site.

5. Make designs for sculpture that would work well as playground equipment in a park for children. What materials would be appropriate for such a project?

6. Is all modern sculpture alike? What does it have to say about life in the twentieth century? Why?

156

157 The wood carvers of the Basonge tribe specialized in making masks, and this example is quite typical of their work. The repeating lines suggest an exciting rhythm while they also harmonize with the overall outline of the mask and its facial details. *Basonge Mask*. Africa. Wood incisions filled with whitish clay; late nineteenth to early twentieth centuries. (Photograph courtesy of the University Museum, University of Pennsylvania, Philadelphia)

158 This vase from ancient China shows how a functional vessel can also be a beautiful object. *Jar with Impressed Design*. China. Black clay with ash glaze on the exterior; late Chou Dynasty (about 600 B.C. to 256 B.C.). (Dallas Museum of Fine Arts)

Working in the language of design, some of the most creative people of all time have had no connection at all with the traditional fine arts. Instead, they became involved with ceramics, metalwork, weaving, woodcraft, enameling, and so on. Usually, when we refer to these fields collectively, they are called the crafts.

Generally, a traditional craft involves the exercise of skills used to shape a given material such as clay, textiles, or wood in ways that have been passed on from one generation to another. In the process, carefully studied observation and repeated practice take place until the highest possible standards of accomplishment are achieved.

To be taken seriously as art and not mere artisanship, outstanding pieces of work in the crafts reflect a deliberate effort to be more than simply functional. For example, useful vessels made of clay may be breathtakingly beautiful in shape and color. At the highest levels of accomplishment, all such handcrafts project a profound concern for excellence in creative refinement and expressive power.

Chapter Fourteen

Creativity in the Crafts

The Background

For centuries before the dawn of history, artisans, or anybody else for that matter, made whatever useful objects people needed. Probably at first, utility was the only criterion that had to be satisfied. For example, if a knife could cut reasonably well, that was enough. A jug made of clay and baked in a fire only had to hold some liquid; how it looked was a minor concern.

Perhaps thousands of years passed before someone started to care about color and form. But when that day arrived, the artist-artisan was born. When other people saw the difference, the desire for

Great mastery over metal-tooling techniques was exercised in creating this spectacular silver cup, lavishly encrusted with jewels. *Chalice of Abbot Suger of Saint-Denis.* France. Sardonyx, gold, silver-gilt, gems, and pearls; about 1140. National Gallery of Art, Washington, D.C.; Widener Collection.

aesthetic satisfaction as well as functional effectiveness became important.

Throughout the past and into the Middle Ages and the Renaissance, craft guilds supervised the process of transferring knowledge and skill from one generation to the next. They were able to flourish because they had support in the form of commissions from royalty, the nobility, the Church, municipal bodies, and prosperous private citizens.

During the seventeenth and eighteenth centuries, the decorative handcrafts continued to be highly valued and deeply respected. Skilled designers were encouraged to create the most elegant wares their imagination could produce. As a consequence, they crafted everything from dinner services to jewelry.

In America, when the colonies were first forming, the Puritan ethic placed great premium on living in a very plain fashion. There was no one in the colonies like King Francis I, who had various articles made for his use and enjoyment by the great goldsmith Benvenuto Cellini, or King Louis XIV, who financed the creation of the Gobelins factory outside of Paris for the production of sumptuous tapestries. Nevertheless, during the seventeenth and eighteenth centuries, men and women in America made many things by hand, and they made them with more than mere mechanical skill. As the colonial period was replaced by the emerging federal republic in the nineteenth century, such people continued with their creative efforts. Carved and painted woodenwares, signs for shops, and weather vanes for barns were made by anonymous and itinerant workers who put more feeling and form into what they made than many of their patrons realized at the time. Likewise, a great deal of work in the handcrafts was achieved by the Indians. They had

The art of lacquer application has been practiced by Oriental artist-artisans for over three thousand years. The process is quite lengthy because each piece is built up from many thin layers. Each one is applied individually and allowed to dry from twelve hours to three days. *Rice or Soup Bowls with Trays*. Japan. Lacquer on wood; about 1800. The Campbell Museum Collection, Camden, New Jersey. (Photograph courtesy of the Campbell Museum)

The eighteenth-century porcelain factory at Meissen provided models of elegant ceramic production that were copied far and wide throughout Europe. Johann Joachim Kaendler. *Tureen*. Saxony, Meissen (Germany). Hard-paste porcelain; about 1745. The Campbell Museum Collection, Camden, New Jersey. (Photograph courtesy of The Campbell Museum)

great skills in tooling leather, making baskets, creating clothes, jewelry, and ceramicwares. However, their traditions in handcrafts were practically lost forever when the European invasions almost completely destroyed the various tribal cultures in North America during the period from the sixteenth century to the nineteenth century.

The fine handcrafts tradition in America almost came to an end with the coming of the Industrial Revolution in the latter part of the nineteenth century. With no market for their products, artist-artisans went to work in factories. Potential handcrafters turned their talent to industrial designing, advertising design, and art education. For awhile, it seemed as though the practice of the handcrafts had died. If it wasn't dead, it certainly appeared to be temporarily buried by the vigorous onslaught of the machine age.

The Contemporary Situation

After a long sleep of about a hundred years, activity in the handcrafts started to show signs of life again. The new awakening took place during the period after World War II. It was as though a signal had sounded across the country. Slowly, but surely, damp clay began to be transformed into beautiful ceramicware. Looms all over the country were threaded and fabrics were woven. Students in college art courses were turning pieces of wood on lathes and igniting the tips of blow torches in order to work creatively in metals. A new renaissance of the crafts was in the making.

Where the handcrafts had once been rooted in the traditions of the past, the contemporary artist-artisan looked to the future. Where earlier handcrafters had been aesthetically and creatively naive,

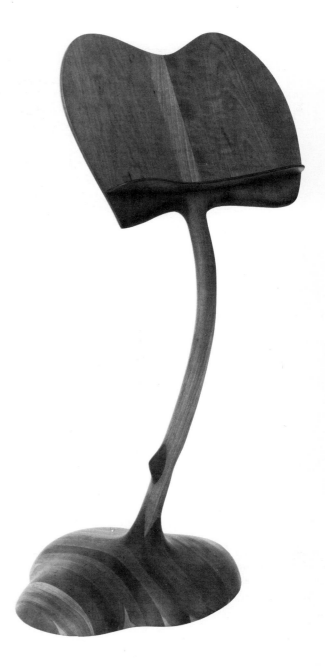

The flying angel weather vane, located on top of a building long ago, must have been a fascinating silhouette seen against the sky. *Angel Weather Vane;* c. 1840. National Gallery of Art, Washington, D.C.; Index of American Design.

Exercising considerable care in his work, Castle has related the overall shape of this object to the rippling character of the wood grain patterns. Wendell Castle. *Music Stand.* Cherry wood; 1972. Philadelphia Museum of Art Collection. (Photograph by A.J. Wyatt, Staff Photographer)

their modern counterparts became as sophisticated as anyone working in the contemporary visual arts. Clearly, the rustic outlook was being replaced by a new cosmopolitanism. Today, the worker in the crafts is very much a part of the twentieth century, in touch with modern poetry, philosophy, and psychology as well as computers, intercontinental travel, and lunar landings. Unlike the craftsmen of the medieval era and the Renaissance, apprenticed early in life to some master tradesman, people active in the crafts today generally have the benefit of a college education (or its equivalent) with major studies in art. Therefore, they identify with contemporary movements, exploring new directions along with others involved creatively in the art world.

Modern artist-artisans use clay, fiber, wood, or metal as media with which to expand their personal horizons. The same urge to explore new ways of vision that led Picasso to structure the human face in a thousand different ways also motivated artists who work in the crafts. They exercise freedom and search for spontaneity as they pursue previously undreamed of approaches to working inventively in form. Now that machines can easily produce all sorts of functional products needed by consumers, the creative handcrafter is free to use his or her material as a visual and tactile medium for intensely personal expression.

It's hard to really understand why but there are those who still insist that the so-called fine arts (such as painting and sculpture) are somehow superior to the crafts. They refuse to admit there can be poor painting and superb weaving, or pathetically empty sculpture and richly compelling jewelry. They fail to see that fine technique is just as essential to a well-made painting as it is to a

A sparkling interplay of colors animates the surface of Murashima's dyed fabric. Kumiko Murashima. Dyed, Printed Textile; 1973. (Photograph courtesy of the artist)

Repeating shapes in different colors generate a lively
rhythm of bright colors in motion. Kumiko Murashima.
Hooked Rug; 1973. (Photograph courtesy of the artist)

well-made weaving. By the same token, they have difficulty understanding that a significant piece of metalwork may have just as much to say aesthetically and expressively whether it is a pitcher or a statue.

Contemporary creative artisans place great importance on the role played by their hands. Invariably, what they make bears the imprint of a human touch because they make products that cannot be easily or inexpensively duplicated by the use of machines. In an era when so much industrial production is geared to built-in obsolescence, the artist-artisan creates forms meant to be kept and treasured for years to come.

This last comment should not be taken to mean that people who work in the crafts view the machine as an enemy. In its early stages, the Industrial Revolution did almost destroy the great handcraft traditions of the past. However, the machines in use today are not likely to be replaced by the artist-artisan. Today, there is a realization that no amount of industrial technology can ever satisfy all the complex emotional and aesthetic needs people have, many of which can only be met by the work of artist-artisans.

Appreciating the Crafts

In working creatively, the artist-artisan begins with an idea for a form. Through an interaction of the idea, the materials, and the techniques of structuring the material, the idea gradually becomes a reality. In the process, the imagination of the artist, guided by past experience and the free play of intuition, constantly evaluates the work in progress. As the piece comes into being, the artist seeks to refine

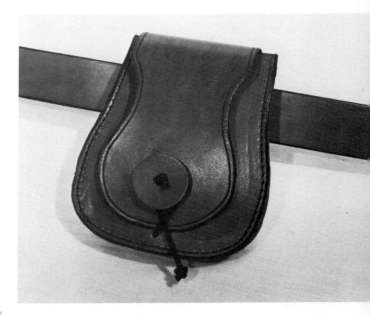

Sturdy construction and simple shapes have been combined here to create an attractive product for daily use. Donna Wescott. *Belt Pouch.* Leather; 1975. (Photograph by Gary Trotta, courtesy of the artist)

Closely related to the use of collage in painting, Rainey's combination of colorful bird feathers and woven yarn identifies a very distinctive personal statement. Sarita Rainey. *Tapestry Weaving.* Yarn and peacock feathers; 1972. (Photograph courtesy of the artist)

168 A combination of metal and mineral become an elegant necklace in this forged silver piece. Madge Allen. *Forged Sterling Silver Necklace with Natural Crystal Quartz Cluster;* 1975. Owned by Mrs. Jessie Campbell, Montclair, New Jersey. (Photograph courtesy of the artist)

169 A sense of simplicity and directness mark Yulman's work in ceramicware. Beverly Yulman. *Stoneware Pot;* 1975. (Photograph courtesy of The Place for Crafts, Bala-Cynwyd, Pennsylvania)

and resolve the original concept until the work is finally completed as perfectly as it possibly can be.

Qualitative creative handcraft is never forced or contrived. Invariably it reflects disciplined control. At the same time, such work also has about it a sense of freshness, a sensitivity of handling, and an air of spontaneity.

Of all the tools used in the various crafts, the most important are the artist's own hands. Directed by the combination of the mind and emotional impulses, the hands are the main channel through which ideas and feelings are transmitted to the materials. In some instances, as for example with clay, the artist's hands can pull, pinch, and poke the material; there is no need to use any additional gadgetry. In other cases, it is the sensitivity with which the artist manipulates handheld tools (such as hammers, needles, saws, files, and so on) that provides the means by which his or her creative intentions transform raw material into a fine finished product.

Ultimately, the success or failure of a handcrafted object depends upon how well it works as a total design. The visual appeal of any given product is just as important as its practical utility. As a matter of fact, the aesthetic dimension of some piece of craftware is quite functional, because people have very real, deep-seated needs for enjoying what they look at.

A major concern of many dedicated artist-artisans is the preservation of the essential integrity of their materials. Wood, for example, has a unique character and a range of working potentials different from anything else. Even when other materials (like laminate plastics) are made to look like wood, they cannot be treated in the same way as wood because their structure is unlike the fibrous nature of wood. Obviously, they can't be carved, sanded, polished, and oiled like a piece of wood. Clearly, the sense of truth inherent in a well-crafted object of wood has a distinctive woody quality all its own. The same principle would apply to articles made from other materials.

Unlike the artisans of the past, modern artists in the crafts put a great deal of importance on originality. Infected with a lively curiosity, a spirit of adventure, and a desire to see what new forms they can invent, they are constantly refreshing and renewing the visual language in their particular discipline. Today, there is no area in which the old vocabulary of craft forms has not been expanded beyond the boundries that existed as recently as a decade ago.

Different artists appoach the formation of their designs in different ways. Some prefer to make rough preliminary sketches followed by more refined drawings of what the finished product should be like. Others prefer to design their forms by working directly in a given material. Because there is no way that is best for all people, each artist evolves a method and style that is right for him or her.

From the outset, all artist-artisans try to achieve harmonious proportions between the different parts of a given object. In a silver ring or a piece of ceramic pottery, the way in which different shapes are brought together results in an agreeable or disagreeable sense of relationship. The same would be true of other articles. As they proceed with their work, artists constantly evaluate the feeling of the forms they are structuring in order to achieve a satisfying appearance in the finished object.

Linear elements are studied in order to see how they may contribute clarity, grace, and unity to a

170

Adell has crafted an impressive piece of jewelry from the simplest of metallic shapes. Carie Adell. *Silver Necklace and Cross;* 1975. Owned by Bishop William Jones. (Photograph by Murray Warren, courtesy of the artist)

172

Light reflected from the metal achieves an extraordinary effect when brightly burning candles stand within the piece. Joe Reyes Apodaca, Jr. *Candelabrum.* Sterling silver; 1966. S.C. Johnson Company Collection of Contemporary Crafts, Racine, Wisconsin. (Photograph courtesy of the S.C. Johnson Company)

In addition to the decorative shape and surface treatment of this ritual candelabrum, the openings above the base lend a spatial richness to the work rarely encountered in fine ceramicware. Fred Manders. *Menorah*. Clay; 1974. (Photograph courtesy of the artist)

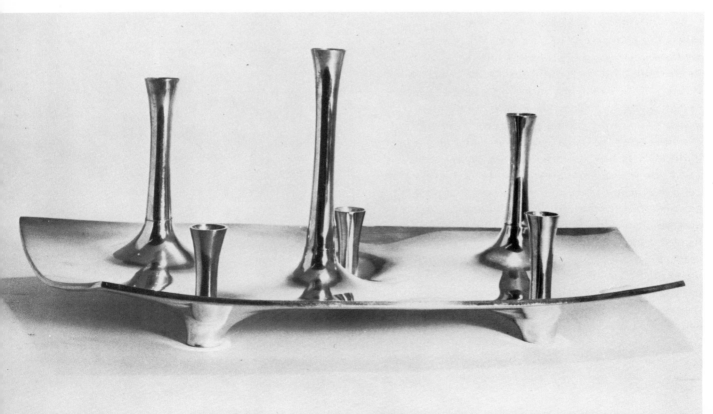

piece of work in progress. Typically, edges of shapes as well as specific lines can give a flow of visual movement, can tie several areas together, can emphasize a particular spot in an object, or can lend definition to the total appearance of a hand-crafted object.

Color and tone are also important design elements used by artist-artisans. Variations in each of these factors will affect the mood and spirit of a piece of work. Obviously, color is a critical design element because everything visible to the eye has some degree of color and tone. Because they are such important factors in the artist's vocabulary of expression, they cannot be left to chance. When color and tone have been used effectively, they add enormously to the quality of a well-crafted product.

Texture refers to the surface characteristics we respond to in what we see and touch. Texture, the relative degrees of smoothness or roughness, affects the appearance of all shapes and colors. In the same vein, texture can suggest feelings of pleasantness and unpleasantness as well as comfort or discomfort. Satisfying, interesting textures can go a long way to increase an article's appeal. By contrast, inappropriate textures or too many "busy" textures can cause us to become irritated and unhappy with an article no matter how well it may have been constructed.

Patterns result from the repetition of some particular shape configuration, such as lines or polka dots. The way pattern functions in the overall design of a handcrafted object is closely related to texture. For this reason, patterns are often introduced for purposes of visual enrichment.

It goes without saying that appearance alone can never be an end in itself whenever a useful product is the artist's goal. Such considerations as conveni-

Modern ceramic artists often find inspiration in plain forms, free of pretension and preciousness. John and Mary Costanza. *Flower and Candle Holder.* Clay with grog; 1972. (Photograph courtesy of the artists)

Manders feels strongly about the need of his forms to function effectively. For example, a spout should pour without dripping. The flat bottom on a pot should not wobble. Fred Manders. *Teapot.* Clay; 1975. (Photograph courtesy of the artist)

173 Using a variety of stitches and an assortment of appliquéd materials, Lesch has structured a bright and colorful collage of cloth and thread. Alma W. Lesch. *Bathsheba's Bedspread.* Stitching and appliqué; 1968. S.C. Johnson Company Collection of Contemporary Crafts, Racine, Wisconsin. (Photograph courtesy of the S.C. Johnson Company)

ence, safety, durability, and ease of maintenance must also be taken into account because, sooner or later, these are going to be matters of concern to a potential consumer.

Naturally, no matter how handsome an object's appearance, it should also fulfill the purpose for which it was created as efficiently as possible. Typically, a silver tray ought to hold its contents without difficulty. Enameled jewelry should enhance a wearer's appearance. A jug meant to hold liquids should not be porous. In short, good design in the creative crafts grows out of a happy marriage between form and function. Both are essential and one should never compromise the integrity of the other.

Of course, all craftwares are not intended to meet purely utilitarian needs. Consider a woven wall hanging. Its main function may be the expression of a personal creative idea. The artist who makes it may be concerned with achieving a sense of designed order and sensuous pleasure in the colors and textures used in making the work. Furthermore, as a satisfying visual object, the piece may also have valuable potentials for providing decorative enrichment to an interior setting. Obviously, besides pleasing the artists who make them, fine craft objects also have a great potential for giving deep satisfaction and aesthetic enjoyment to others. After all is said and done, perhaps this is one of the most significant functions a work of art may ever be called upon to fulfill.

ACTIVITIES TO EXPLORE:

1. Visit the studio of an artist-artisan in your community who works in one of the creative crafts. See what insights you can develop into this person's creative efforts.

2. Do you think most people you know have any interest in handcrafted wares? What accounts for their interest or lack of interest? Discuss these questions with people in your class.

3. Visit a shop in your community where creative crafts are displayed and sold. If you could afford to buy anything there you want, what would you like to have? Why?

4. With the cooperation of your art teacher, make a piece of jewelry from some inexpensive material which you can give to someone you like as a gift.

5. If you could pursue a professional career in one field of the crafts, which area would you choose? Consider the following possibilities: ceramics, woodworking, metalworking, making mosaics, weaving, macrame, textile dying and printing, stained glass, enameling, jewelry making, glass blowing, leathercraft, and working in plastics.

6. Make believe you are an advertising agency executive responsible for preparing a magazine advertisement urging people to buy handcrafted wares. What important points would you include in your message? What visuals would you include? Why?

The two woven figures consist of wood and synthetics in a tube weave, finished by stuffing the forms with acrylic fibers. Jean Stamsta. *Wild Sister and The Other Brother*. Wool and synthetic Fibers; 1968–1969. S.C. Johnson Company Collection of Contemporary Crafts, Racine, Wisconsin. (Photograph courtesy of the S.C. Johnson Company)

Through their work, artists share a richness of creative vision with the world. (Photograph of Alberto Giacometti
by Ernst Scheidegger, courtesy of Pro Helvetia, Zurich,
Switzerland)

As you spend time with art, you realize how satisfying such experience can be. It's uncanny how alive and enriched you become when you're involved this way. As you look at different things, try to see how effects are achieved—how the elements of design have been put together to produce an impact on your sensibilities. Ask yourself what the artist did to express a composite of ideas and feelings in a vocabulary of visual form. The more you search, the more you will come to understand.

Art Appreciation is Personal

Just as artists are all different from each other so are people when they become spectators in the art scene. After all, nobody in the world ever sees exactly what you see with your own eyes. No one else can feel precisely the same way you do. No other people can possibly duplicate in their mind what you know at any single moment in time. That is why encounters with art are such valuable self-actualizing experiences. Furthermore, one of the most important insights you acquire in learning about art is the realization that instant appreciation is neither possible nor especially desirable. *It takes time to learn how to see and feel in depth*. To be genuinely significant in your life, the capacity for appreciation has to be cultivated slowly.

As suggested earlier, it is especially helpful to develop an awareness of what is around you in your daily life. Before evaluations of sophisticated art objects are undertaken, see how responsive you can become to the presence of design in nature; to the play of light and shadows on all sorts of surfaces; to the colors, textures, and patterns you find in clothing, home furnishings, and the whole spectrum of industrially produced objects that surround you all the time.

Chapter Fifteen

Toward Deeper Understanding

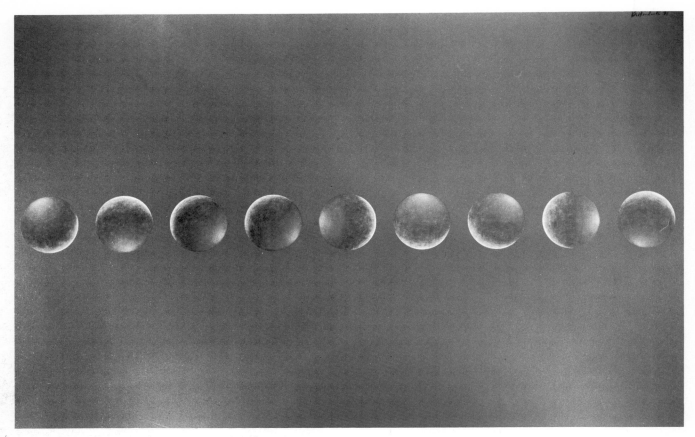

178 Form is where you find it. The flight of a ball through space took hold of Barkely Hendricks's attention. After reflecting on what he saw, he made a painting to preserve his insights on canvas. Now they are there for others to also see and enjoy. *Top Heavy*. Barkley Hendricks. (Photograph courtesy of the artist)

174 The orderly structure of plant leaves provides a beautiful example of design in nature. (Photograph by Ernie Leven)

The Language of Design

The most basic necessity for meaningful art appreciation is familiarity with the grammar and vocabulary of visual design. More than any other factor, a sense of order is basic to design. Without order, there can be no design. Both the world of nature and the history of art provide countless examples to support this viewpoint. For example, consider the structure of a leaf. The overall form is organized to encourage the best possible life for the leaf within the limits of its existence. In short, a leaf is a superbly ordered botanical design. By the same token, a complete interrelated sense of organized structure is always evident in outstanding works of art. Of course, it is important to remember that the presence of orderly design relationships does not automatically make for greatness in a work of art. The investment of personal dedication and an intensity of feeling are equally important. However, without a solid sense of visual organization, no piece of work is likely to ever become especially significant as art.

In a successful art object, everything counts. *What* is said is dependent upon *how* it is said. The artist who aims to make a worthwhile creative contribution must pay careful attention to materials and how they are handled. Style and expressive content have to be woven together as one whole fabric. When all the parts are thus joined, a first-rate accomplishment may emerge.

Art as an object is therefore a direct result of art as a process; a process not merely of manipulating materials inventively but also of exercising intuition and framing goals, emotionally and intellectually. Making art is a complex activity rising out of deep internal urges demanding realization in concrete form. As the process evolves, judgments are constantly made regarding the appearance of a piece of work that has been started. Until the work is done, the artist often feels quite restless. At times, the tension can be almost maddening. But when the elements of expressive compulsion and imaginative drive are finally joined in a satisfactory conclusion, the artist often experiences enormous satisfaction and enjoys a sense of great accomplishment.

Now, It's Up to You

As a result of reading this book, you have a better idea of what to look for when you see art than you had before. How much more you get from art will depend upon the further interest, concentration, and contact you bring to the subject. Without a doubt, the more of yourself you put in, the more you are likely to take away.

In addition to looking at art appreciatively, try participating actively in making art yourself. For example, pick up a brush and some paint. See what you can do with them in your own distinctive way. Everything you've learned here will make these materials mean more to you than they did before.

Explore what design and expression are about in all sorts of ways. Besides painting, try drawing, design, sculpture, printmaking, architecture, and crafts; if not all at once, then one by one. Feel what living with art is all about. Enjoy the exhilaration that comes from working creatively in a personal language of visual form.

Feel free to reach out and get in touch with art. You will always be the richer for doing so. Getting deeper and deeper into art is a little like flying above the earth. The higher you go, the more you see. Increasingly, the impact made upon you by art will become more and more a part of you. No one can ever take it away. For the rest of your life, it's yours.

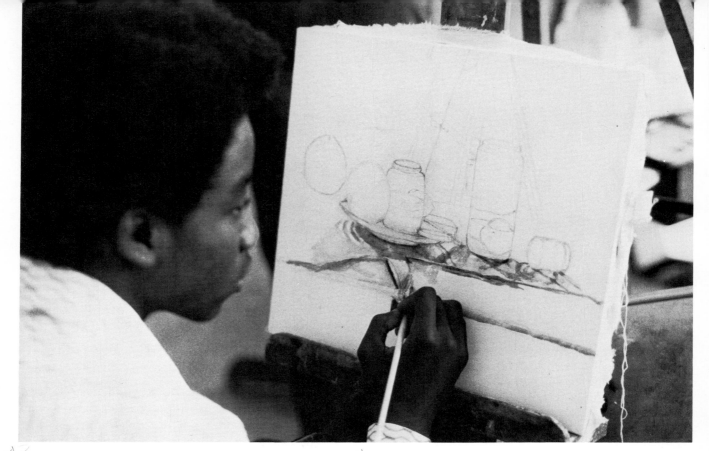

180 Nothing else in the world is quite like getting involved with art in your own special way. (Photograph courtesy of George Horn, Baltimore Public Schools)

181 High school students here are working creatively in art. (Photograph courtesy of George Horn, Baltimore Public Schools)

GLOSSARY

Aerial perspective   Creating the effect of distance on a flat surface, by using cold pale colors for distant features, such as a range of hills and the sky behind them in a landscape.

Aesthetics   The branch of philosophy dealing with the study of form and meaning in works of art.

Aquarelle   Painting with water soluble media.

Arch   Almost any curved structural member used to span space.

Atelier   A workshop or studio where art is made.

Barbizon school   From the village of that name on the outskirts of the Forest of Fontainbleau in France. The aim of the painters who lived and worked there since 1830 was to portray nature as a living dynamic force.

Body colors   Pigments (oil or watercolors) which have body or opacity, as opposed to those that are transparent.

Byzantine art   Art of the eastern Roman Empire associated with the reign of the emperor Justinian and the style of pictorial representation established by the mosaics in the Hagia Sophia Church at Istanbul. The influence of this style extended throughout Europe for over a thousand years, especially in the form of religious icon painting.

Calligraphy   The art of ornamental penmanship or—in Chinese and Japanese writing especially—brushwork. Drawings and paintings are said to be calligraphic when they are essentially linear, resembling the spontaneous line and accents of handwriting.

Cantilever   A beam or slab projecting a considerable distance beyond a post or a wall. This technique enjoys considerable favor among many modern architects.

Caricature   A representation of a person or object based upon the overemphasis or exaggeration of characteristic traits.

Chiaroscuro   Gradations of light and dark within a picture, in which the forms are largely determined by the meeting of lighter and darker areas.

Color   Color has three qualities: *hue*—the actual color itself, for example, red, yellow, blue, and so on; *chroma*—the relative brilliance or intensity of a color, for example, bright or dull red; *value*—the lightness or darkness of a color.

Column   A cylindrical upright or pillar, usually used in a row in order to carry (support) a load in architecture.

Composition   The organization of design elements in a work of art.

Contour   The outline of a form, especially when it suggests a volume or a mass.

Cromlech   A prehistoric monument formed of great stones set on end and arranged in a circle, as at Stonehenge.

Design   The plan or general concept of a work of art.

Drypoint   A method of printmaking in which lines are scratched directly into a plate with a sharp instrument.

Earth colors   Pigments, such as yellow ochre, terra verte, and umber, which are obtained by mining them from the earth. They owe their color to the presence of compounds of iron and closely associated metals like manganese.

Enamel (enameling)   A process of applying ground glass substances of various colors to metallic or porcelain surfaces.

Encaustic   A technique in which pigments are mixed with molten wax and applied to a painting surface with warmed instruments.

Engraving   The craft of working a design into wood or metal with sharp tools. Usually, the material thus treated serves as a matrix from which graphic prints may then be made.

Etching   A method of preparing a metal plate, such as zinc, copper, or steel, from which graphic prints are then made. The design is first drawn into a wax ground with an etching needle and then subjected to a series of acid bitings. Finally the plate is inked, wiped, and printed.

Etruscan art   The art produced by the people of Etruria in Northern Italy around the sixth century B.C. Strongly influenced by the Greeks, the Etruscan civilization and culture were eventually absorbed into the Roman Empire.

Fixative   a solution sprayed on drawings done with charcoal, pencil, chalk, and various other impermanent materials so as to prevent smudging.

Foreshortening   A method of representing objects or parts of objects as if they were seen at an angle and receding into space instead of being seen in a strictly frontal or profile view.

180

Form The structural element(s) in a work of art by which the artist's conception is given a tangible form.

Genre The protrayal of subject matter from everyday life, such as domestic and humorous scenes.

Gilding The craft of covering substances, such as wood, with layers of gold.

Glaze
1. A glassy coat applied to pottery to seal and color it.
2. A thin transparent or semitransparent film of paint brushed over another layer of paint, allowing it to show through and usually altering its color.

Gouache A technique of painting with opaque colors which have been ground in water and tempered with a preparation of gum. Also, a term used to describe a method of watercolor painting in which white is used as a pigment, by contrast with the method of attaining whites by allowing the paper to show through.

Icon An Eastern Church image, painting, or mosaic of a sacred personage, regarded as sacred in itself.

Iconography The language of symbols, images, and pictures. Also, the representation of abstract ideas through a system of symbolic imagery.

Illumination Painting on parchment which acts as an adornment for the accompanying manuscript. The effect is often heightened by the use of gold leaf.

Impasto A particularly thick or heavy application of paint.

Lithography A method of printmaking in which a drawing is made on a lithographic stone or a prepared zinc plate with a greasy crayon, or ink, and prints taken. For color lithography, separate drawings are required for each color.

Maquette A rough miniature model used by sculptors as a guide for a larger finished work.

Mannerism Originally implied a superficial imitation of a great creative style, lacking in originality or deep feeling. Now it is used to define a period of originality and diversity which followed on the heels of the high Renaissance in Italy and lasted through the rest of the sixteenth century.

Medium In a general sense, the particular material with which an artwork is executed—oils, watercolor, chalks, pen and ink, and so on. It may also refer to the liquid with which powdered pigments are ground to make paint.

Mosaic Designs or pictures formed from small chips of glass, stone, marble, or other materials. The technique was used in Roman times for floor and wall decorations and was extensively used by Byzantine artists to picture the story of Christianity.

Mural painting A decorative picture painted on a wall or fastened to a wall surface.

Palette The surface on which artists place and mix their paints and also the range of colors they use.

Papiers collés (Collage) From the French, meaning "pasted papers." The making of pictures and designs from pieces of colored paper, cardboard, newsprint, playing cards, and so on, which are cut into various shapes and attached to paper, board, or canvas.

Pastel Powdered pigments mixed with gum and formed into sticks of chalk for drawing. Pastels are usually so broadly applied over the entire surface of the paper that the effect resembles oil painting, although the colors are generally rather pale.

Perspective The representation on a two-dimensional surface of three-dimensional objects in space.

Pigments The coloring substances, usually in powder form, which are ground with liquids, called vehicles, to form paint.

Pre-Columbian art The art of the Americas before the coming of European settlers.

Primary colors The three basic hues—red, yellow, and blue—from which, theoretically, all others can be mixed.

Representational art The kind of expressive form which aims to reproduce the physical appearance of people, places, and things. This is the opposite of nonrepresentational art where no subject matter appears.

Sfumato The delicate blending of light tones into dark as in a smokey haze. Leonardo da Vinci was one of the great exponents of this practice.

Sgraffito A method of decoration in which a dark surface which has been covered by a coat of lighter color is made to reappear by scratching away the light colored overpainting.

Shade A term used to designate a color mixed with black.

Silk screen A method of making original graphic prints by using stencils attached to silk stretched tightly on a frame.

Sketch A rapid drawing or painting, which may be complete in itself or intended as a preliminary study for a more detailed project.

Stained glass The craft of cutting colored glass into various shapes, joined by lead strips to form a pictorial window design. The technique was in widespread use during the medieval era.

Symmetry The harmonious balancing of design elements in a composition.

Techniques In art, the mastery of methods and materials used in a specific working process.

Tempera A method of painting in which pigments ground in water are mixed or tempered with an emulsion of egg yolk. The word is also used for an opaque water-soluble paint made of pigment and gum arabic.

Triptych   A painting in the form of three panels, hinged together, frequently seen in religious (altarpiece) works of art.

Trompe L'Oeil   A French term meaning a very illusionistic rendering of subject matter that tricks a spectator's eye into thinking it sees something that actually isn't there, such as drops of dew painted on a picture of a rose petal. Literally, the words mean "to deceive the eye."

Wash   In painting, especially watercolor and brush drawing, a broad thin film of highly diluted pigment.

Watercolor   Pigments mixed with a water-soluble gum, usually applied in broad washes on white paper.

Woodcut   A graphic print made from a design cut into a wooden block. All parts of the design which are not to be printed are cut away with knives and gouges.

SUGGESTED BOOKS FOR FURTHER READING

General Appreciation — Art and Design in Everyday Life

America's Arts and Skills. Edited by the editors of Life Magazine. New York: E. P. Dutton & Co., Inc., 1957.

Anderson, Donald M. *Elements of Design.* New York: Holt, Rinehart and Winston, Inc., 1961.

Arnheim, Rudolf. *Art and Visual Perception.* Berkeley, Cal.: University of California Press, 1954.

Bauhaus: 1919–1928. Edited by Walter Gropius. New York: Museum of Modern Art, 1938.

Benthall, Jonathan. *Science and Technology in Art Today.* New York: Praeger Publishers, Inc., 1972.

Clark, Sir Kenneth. *Civilization: A Personal View.* New York: Harper & Row, Publishers, 1969.

Faulkner, Ray, and Ziegfeld, Edwin. *Art Today: An Introduction to the Visual Arts.* 5th ed. rev. New York: Holt, Rinehart and Winston, Inc., 1969.

Feldman, Edmund Burke, *Varieties of Visual Exprience: Art as Image and Idea.* 2d ed. Englewood Cliffs, N.J.: Prentice-Hall, Inc., 1971.

Gombrich, Ernest H. *The Story of Art.* 12th ed. rev. London: Phaidon, 1972.

Industrial Design in America. Edited by the Society of Industrial Designers. New York: Farrar, Straus and Young Inc. (Annual Publication.)

Itten, Johannes. *Design and Form: The Basic Course at the Bauhaus.* New York: Reinhold Publishing Corp., 1964.

Janson, H. W. *History of Art.* Rev. ed. Englewood Cliffs, N.J.: Prentice-Hall and Abrams, 1969.

Kepes, Gyorgy. *The Language of Vision.* Chicago: Theobald, 1945.

Knobler, Nathan. *The Visual Dialogue.* 2d ed. New York: Holt, Rinehart and Winston, Inc., 1968.

Kramrisch, Stella. *The Art of India.* 3d ed. New York: Phaidon, 1965.

Lee, Sherman. *A History of Far Eastern Art.* Englewood Cliffs, N.J., and New York: Prentice-Hall and Abrams, 1964.

Papanek, Victor. *Design for the Real World.* New York: Bantam Books, Inc., 1973.

Read, Sir Herbert. *Art and Society.* London: Faber and Faber, 1950.

Environmental Planning and Renewal

Bacon, Edmund N. *Design of Cities.* New York: The Viking Press, Inc., 1967.

Blake, Peter. *God's Own Junkyard.* New York: Holt, Rinehart and Winston, Inc., 1964.

Jacobs, Jane. *The Death and Life of Great American Cities.* New York: Vintage Books, Random House, Inc., 1963.

Johnson-Marshall, Percy. *Rebuilding Cities.* Chicago: Aldine Publishing Company, 1966.

Le Corbusier. *The City of Tomorrow.* London: Architectural Press, 1947.

Mc Harg, Ian L. *Design with Nature.* Garden City, N.Y.: Doubleday & Company, Inc., 1971.

Neutra, Richard J. *Survival Through Design.* New York: Oxford University Press, 1954.

Safdie, Moshe. *Beyond Habitat.* Cambridge, Mass.: M.I.T. Press, 1973.

Stein, Charles S. *Toward New Towns for America.* Cambridge, Mass: M.I.T. Press, 1966.

Architecture of the Past

Alex, William. *Japanese Architecture.* New York: George Braziller, Inc., 1963.

Collins, Peter. *Changing Ideals in Modern Architecture, 1750–1950.* London: Faber and Faber, 1965.

Fakhry, Ahmed. *The Pyramids.* Chicago; University of Chicago Press, 1962.

Jantzen, Hans. *High Gothic: The Classic Cathedrals of Chartres, Reims, Amiens.* Translated by James Palmes. New York: Pantheon Books, Inc., 1962.

Millon, Henry A. *Baroque and Rococo Architecture.* New York: George Braziller, Inc., 1961.

Murray, Peter. *The Architecture of the Italian Renaissance.* New York: Schocken Books, Inc., 1966.

Pevsner, Nikolaus. *An Outline of European Architecture.* 6th (jubilee) ed. Baltimore: Penguin Books, Inc., 1960.

Rudofsky, Bernard. *Architecture Without Architects.* Garden City, N.Y.: Doubleday & Company, Inc., 1964.

Saalman, Howard. *Medieval Architecture.* New York: George Braziller, Inc., 1962.

Simson, von, Otto G. *The Gothic Cathedral.* New York: Pantheon Books, Inc., 1956.

Wittkower, Rudolf. *Art and Architecture in Italy, 1600–1750.* Pelican History of Art. Baltimore: Penguin Books, Inc., 1958.

Modern Architecture

Bitterman, Eleanor. *Art in Modern Architecture.* New York: Reinhold Publishing Corp., 1952.

Blake, Peter. *Le Corbusier.* Baltimore: Penguin Books, Inc., 1964.

Conrads, Ulrich, and Sperlich, Hans. *The Architecture of Fantasy.* New York: Frederick A. Praeger, Inc., 1962.

Cook, Peter. *Experimental Architecture.* New York: Universe Books, 1970.

Drew, Philip. *Third Generation: The Changing Meaning of Architecture.* New York: Praeger Publishers, Inc., 1972.

Drexler, Arthur. *Mies Van Der Rohe.* New York: George Braziller, Inc., 1960.

Encyclopedia of Modern Architecture. Edited by Wolfgang Pehnt. New York: Harry N. Abrams, Inc., 1964.

Fuller, Buckminster R., and Marks, Robert. *The Dymaxion World of Buckminster Fuller.* Garden City, N.Y.: Doubleday/Anchor Press, 1973.

Gropius, Walter. *The New Architecture and the Bauhaus.* Boston: Charles T. Branford Company, 1937.

Hall, Edward. *The Hidden Dimension.* Garden City, N.Y.: Doubleday/Anchor Press, 1969.

Halprin, Lawrence. *The RSVP Cycles—Creative Processes in the Human Environment.* New York: George Braziller, Inc., 1969.

Heyer, Paul. *Architects On Architecture.* New York: Walker & Company, 1966.

Jencks, Charles. *Modern Movement in Architecture.* Garden City, N.Y.: Doubleday/*Anchor Press*, 1973.

Lynch, Kevin. *The Image of the City.* Cambridge, Mass.: M.I.T. Press, 1960.

McHale, John. *The Future of the Future.* New York: Ballantine Books, Inc., 1971.

Negroponte, Nicholas. *The Architecture Machine.* Cambridge, Mass.: M.I.T. Press, 1970.

Schwartz, Eugene S. *Overskill.* New York: Ballantine Books, Inc., 1972.

Scully, Vincent. *American Architecture and Urbanism.* New York: Praeger Publishers, Inc., 1969.

Stern, Robert. *New Directions in American Architecture.* New York: George Braziller, Inc., 1969.

Tunnard, Christopher. *The City of Man.* New York: Charles Scribner's Sons, 1953.

Venturi, Robert. *Complexity and Contradiction in Architecture.* New York: Museum of Modern Art, 1966.

Wall, D. *Visionary Cities: The Arcology of Paolo Soleri.* New York: Praeger Publishers, Inc., 1970.

Weisskamp, Herbert. *Beautiful Homes and Gardens in California.* New York: Harry N. Abrams, Inc., 1964.

Wright, Frank L. *The Natural House.* New York: Horizon Press, 1958.

Painting of the Past

Arias, Paolo E., and Hirmer, Max. A History of 1000 Years of Greek Vase Painting. New York: Harry N. Abrams, Inc., 1963.

Beckwith, John. *Early Medieval Art.* New York: Praeger Publishers, Inc., 1964.

Demargne, Pierre. *Aegean Art: The Origins of Greek Art.* Translated by Stuart Gilbert and James Emmons. New York: Golden Press, 1964.

Dupont, J., and Gnudi, C. *Gothic Painting.* New York: Skira, 1954.

Eliot, Alexander. *Three Hundred Years of American Painting.* New York: Time, Inc., 1957.

Grazioli, Paolo. *Paleolithic Art.* New York: McGraw-Hill Book Company, 1960.

Hanfmann, George M. A. *Roman Art.* Greenwich, Conn.: New York Graphic Society, 1964.

Hartt, Frederick. *History of Italian Renaissance Art.* New York: Harry N. Abrams, Inc., 1969.

Homer, W. I. *Seurat and the Science of Painting.* Cambridge, Mass: M.I.T. Press, 1964.

McCoubrey, John. *American Art, 1700–1960, Sources and Documents in the History of Art.* Englewood Cliffs, N.J.: Prentice-Hall, Inc., 1965.

Michalowski, Kazimierz. *Art of Ancient Egypt.* New York: Harry N. Abrams, Inc., 1969.

Pfuhl, Ernst. *Masterpieces of Greek Drawing and Painting.* Translated by Sir John Beazley. Latest ed. New York: Macmillan, Inc., 1955.

Rewald, John. *The History of Impressionism.* Rev. ed. New York: Museum of Modern Art, 1961.

———. *Post-Impressionism from van Gogh to Gaugin.* 2d ed. New York: Museum of Modern Art, 1962.

Rice, David Talbot. *Art of the Byzantine Era.* New York, Praeger Publishers, Inc., 1963.

van Gogh, Vincent. *Complete Letters.* Translated by Mrs. J. van Gogh-Bonger and C. de Dood. 2d ed. 3 vols. Greenwich, Conn.: New York Graphic Society, 1959.

Vasari, Giorgio. *The Lives of the Painters, Sculptors, and Architects.* Translated by A. B. Hind. 4 vols. New York: E. P. Dutton & Co., Inc., 1927.

Waterhouse, Ellis K. *Painting in Britain, 1530–1790.* 2d ed. Pelican History of Art. Baltimore: Penguin Books, Inc., 1962.

Modern Painting

Alloway, Lawrence. *American Pop Art*. New York: Collier Books, 1974.

Arnason, H. H. *History of Modern Art*. New York: Harry N. Abrams, Inc., 1968.

Ashton, Dore. *The New York School*. New York: The Viking Press, Inc., 1973.

Barr, Alfred H., Jr. *Matisse: His Art and His Public*. New York: Museum of Modern Art, 1951.

———. *Picasso: Fifty Years of His Art*. New York: Museum of Modern Art, 1946.

Barrett, Cyril. *An Introduction to Optical Art*. New York: E. P. Dutton & Co., Inc., 1971.

Battcock, Gregory, ed. *Minimal Art: A Critical Anthology*. New York: E. P. Dutton & Co., Inc., 1968.

Brown, Milton. *American Painting from the Armory Show to the Depression*. Princeton, N.J.: Princeton University Press, 1955.

Cummings, Paul. *A Dictionary of Contemporary American Artists*. 2d ed. New York: St. Martin's Press, Inc., 1971.

Duthuit, Georges. *The Fauvist Painters*. New York: George Wittenborn, Inc., 1950.

Finch, Christopher. *Pop Art: The Object and the Image*. New York: E. P. Dutton & Co., Inc., 1968.

Geldzahler, Henry, ed. *New York Painting and Sculpture, 1940–1970*. New York: E. P. Dutton & Co., Inc., 1969.

Haftmann, Werner. *Painting in the Twentieth Century*. 2 vols. New York: Praeger Publishers, Inc., 1961.

Henri, Robert. *The Art Spirit*. Compiled by Margery Ryerson. Rev. ed. Philadelphia: J. B. Lippincott Company, 1951. Reflects the New York Studio and classroom scene in the earlier part of the century.

Hess, T. B. *Abstract Painting: Background and American Phase*. New York: The Viking Press, Inc., 1951.

Hunter, Sam. *American Art of the 20th Century*. New York: Harry N. Abrams, Inc., 1972.

Jaffé, Hans L. C. *De Stijl, 1917–1931; The Dutch Contribution to Modern Art*. Amsterdam; Meulenhoff, 1956.

Kandinsky, Wassily. *Concerning the Spiritual in Art, and Painting in Particular*. Translated by M. Sadleir. New York: George Wittenborn, Inc., 1964.

Klee, Paul. *On Modern Art*. Translated by P. Findlay. London: Faber and Faber, 1948.

———. *Pedagogical Sketchbook*. Translated by S. Peech. New York: Prager Publishers, Inc., 1960.

Lake, Carleton, and Maillard, Robert, eds. *A Dictionary of Modern Painting*. 3d ed. London: Methuen, 1964.

Larkin, Oliver. *Art and Life in America*, New York: Rinehart, 1949.

Motherwell, Robert. *The Dada Painters and Poets*. New York: Wittenborn, Schultz, 1951.

Penrose, Sir Roland. *Picasso: His Life and Work*. Rev. ed. New York: Harper & Row, Publishers, 1973.

Richter, Hans. *Dada: Art and Anti-Art*. New York: McGraw-Hill Book Company, 1965.

Rickey, George. *Constructivism: Origins and Evolution*. New York: George Braziller, Inc. 1967.

Rosenberg, Harold. *The Anxious Object: Art Today and Its Audience*. New York: Horizon Press, 1964.

Rosenblum, Robert. *Cubism and Twentieth-Century Art*. New York: Harry N. Abrams, Inc., 1961.

Rubin, William S. *Dada, Surrealism, and Their Heritage*. New York: Musuem of Modern Art, 1968.

Russell, John, and Gablik, Suzi. *Pop Art Redefined*. New York: Prager Publishers, Inc., 1969.

Scharf, Aaron. *Art and Photography*. Baltimore: Allen Lane, 1969.

Selz, Peter. *German Expressionist Painting*. Berkeley, Col.: University of California Press, 1957.

———. *New Image of Man*. New York: Museum of Modern Art, 1959.

Seuphor, Michel. *Dictionary of Abstract Painting with a History of Abstract Painting*. New York: Tudor, 1957.

Smith, Edward Lucie. *Late Modern, The Visual Arts Since 1945*. New York: Praeger Publishers, Inc., 1969.

Wasserman, Burton. *Modern Painting: The Movements, The Artists, Their Work*. Worcester, Mass.: Davis Publications, Inc., 1970.

Drawing and Original Graphic Prints

Biegeleisen, J. I. *Screen Printing*. New York: Watson-Guptill, 1971.

Buckland-Wright, John. *Engraving and Etching: Techniques and the Modern Trend*. London: The Studio Limited, 1953.

Hayter, S. W. *New Ways of Gravure*. London: Routledge and Kegan Paul, 1949.

Heller, Jules. *Printmaking Today*. New York: Holt, Rinehart and Winston, Inc., 1958.

Hind, Arthur M. *History of Engraving and Etching*. 3d rev. ed. Boston: Houghton Mifflin Company, 1927.

———. *An Introduction to a History of Woodcut*. Boston: Houghton Mifflin Company, 1935.

Ivins, William M., Jr. *How Prints Look*. New York: Metropolitan Museum of Art, 1943.

Mayor, A. Hyatt. *Prints and People*. New York: Metropolitan Museum of Art, 1971.

Mendelowitz, Daniel M. *Drawing*. New York: Holt, Rinehart and Winston, Inc., 1966.

Nicolaides, Kimon. *The Natural Way to Draw*. Boston: Houghton Mifflin Company, 1941.

Peterdi, Gabor. *Printmaking: Methods Old and New.* New York: Macmillan, Inc., 1959.

Romano, Clare, and Ross, John. *The Complete Printmaker.* New York: The Free Press, 1972.

Stubbe, Wolf. *Graphic Arts in the Twentieth Century.* New York: Frederick A. Praeger, Inc., 1963.

Zigrosser, Carl, ed. *Prints.* New York: Holt, Rinehart, and Winston, Inc., 1962.

Sculpture from the Past

Adam, Sheila. *The Technique of Greek Sculpture in the Archaic and Classical Periods.* London: Thames & Hudson, 1967.

Crichton, George H., *Romanesque Sculpture in Italy,* London: Routledge and Kegan Paul, 1954.

Friedlaender, Walter F. *Michelangelo: The Complete Sculpture.* New York: Harry N. Abrams, Inc., 1969.

Katzenellenbogen, Adolf. *The Sculptural Programs of Chartres Cathedral.* Baltimore: The Johns Hopkins University Press, 1959.

Lullies, Reinhard, and Hirmer, Max. *Greek Sculpture.* New York: Harry N. Abrams, Inc., 1960.

Pope-Hennessy, John. *Italian Gothic Sculpture.* London: Phaidon, 1955.

———. *Italian High Renaissance and Baroque Sculpture.* 3 vols. London: Phaidon, 1963.

Richter, Gisela M. A. *The Sculpture and Sculptors of the Greeks.* New rev. ed. New Haven, Conn.: Yale University Press, 1950.

Wingert, Paul S. *The Sculpture of Negro Africa.* New York: Columbia University Press, 1959.

Modern Sculpture

Elsen, Albert Edward. *Rodin.* Garden City, N.Y.: for the Museum of Modern Art, 1963.

Hammacher, A. M. *Evolution of Modern Sculpture: Tradition and Innovation.* New York: Harry N. Abrams, Inc., 1969.

Henri, Adrian. *Total Art: Environments, Happenings and Performance.* New York: Praeger Publishers, Inc., 1974.

Kelly, James J. *The Sculptural Idea.* Minneapolis: Burgess, 1970. A handy introduction to aspects of modern sculpture.

Licht, Fred S. *Sculpture of the 19th and 20th Centuries.* Greenwich, Conn.: New York Graphic Society, 1967.

Maillard, Robert, ed. *New Dictionary of Modern Sculpture.* New York: Tudor, 1971.

Mills, John W. *The Technique of Sculpture.* New York: Van Nostrand Reinhold Publishing Corp., 1965.

Oldenburg, Claes. *Proposals for Monuments and Buildings.* Chicago: Big Table Publishing Co., 1969.

Popper, Frank. *Origins and Development of Kinetic Art.* Greenwich, Conn: New York Graphic Society, 1968.

Read, Sir Herbert. *A Concise History of Contemporary Sculpture.* New York: Praeger Publishers, Inc., 1964.

Rickey, George. *Constructivism Origins and Evolution.* New York: George Braziller, Inc., 1967.

Seitz, William C. *The Art of Assemblage.* New York: Museum of Modern Art, 1961.

Selz, Jean. *Modern Sculpture, Origins and Evolution.* Translated by Annette Michelson. New York: George Braziller, Inc., 1963.

The Creative Crafts

A Treasury of Scandinavian Design. Edited by Erik Kahle. New York: Golden Press, Inc., 1961.

Christensen, Erwin W. *Primitive Art.* New York: Crown Publishers, Inc., 1955.

Leiris, Michel, and Delange, Jacqueline. *African Art.* New York: Golden Press, Inc., 1968.

Linton, Ralph, and Wingert, Paul S. *Arts of the South Seas.* New York: Museum of Modern Art, 1946.

Mattil, Edward L. *Meaning in Crafts.* 2d ed. Englewood Cliffs, N.J.: Prentice-Hall, Inc., 1965.

Miles, Charles. *Indian and Eskimo Artifacts of North America.* Chicago: Henry Regnery Co., 1963.

Nordness, Lee. *Objects: USA.* New York: The Viking Press, Inc., 1970.

Schneider, Richard C. *Crafts of the North American Indians.* New York: Van Nostrand Reinhold Company, 1972.

Williams, Christopher. *Craftsmen of Necessity.* New York: Vintage Books, 1974.

Resources for Art Appreciation

Multicolor Slides

The following museums sell 35-mm full-color slides. Contact them at the addresses noted here to obtain a copy of their current catalog.

Slide Library
Philadelphia Museum of Art
Benjamin Franklin Parkway
Philadelphia, Pennsylvania 19130

Color Slide Department
Detroit Institute of Arts
5200 Woodard Avenue
Detroit, Michigan 48202

Museum Store
The Art Institute of Chicago
Chicago, Illinois 60603

Publications Sales
The Museum of Modern Art
11 West 53rd Street
New York, New York 10019

Publications Department
National Gallery of Art
Washington, D.C. 20565

The Metropolitan Museum of Art
Slide Sales Department
Fifth Avenue and 82nd Street
New York, New York 10028

Publications Department
The Newark Museum
43-49 Washington Street
Newark, New Jersey 07101

The Solomon Guggenheim Museum
1071 Fifth Avenue
New York, New York 10028

The following commercial organizations sell 35-mm full-color slides.

Amco, Inc.
Box 218
Port Richey, Florida 33568

American Library
Color Slide Company Inc.
305 East 45th Street
New York, New York 10017

American Craftsmen's Council
29 West 52nd Street
New York, New York 10019
Attention: AV Librarian

Art Council Aids
Box 641
Beverly Hills, California 90213

Block Color Reproductions
1309 North Genessee Avenue
Hollywood, California 90028

Cultural History Research, Inc.
Harrison, New York 10528

Dr. Konrad Prothman
2787 Milburn Avenue
Baldwin, New York 11510

Color Slide Program of World's Art
McGraw-Hill Book Company
P.O. Box 582
Hightstown, New Jersey 08520

Sandak Inc.
180 Harvard Avenue
Stamford, Connecticut 06902

Society of French American Cultural
Services and Educational Aid
Audio-Visual Department
972 Fifth Avenue
New York, New York 10021

Barney Burstein
29 Commonwealth Avenue
Boston, Massachusetts 02116

Scala Fine Arts Publishers, Incorporated
28 West 44th Street
New York, New York 10036

Slides for Education
5574 Lakewood Avenue
Detroit, Michigan 48213

European Art Color Slides
20 West 70th Street
New York, New York 10023

Budek Slides
P.O. Box 4309
East Providence, Rhode Island 02914

Small Multicolor Reproductions

The University Prints
21 East Street
Winchester, Massachusetts 01890

Barton-Cotton
Sales Department
1405 Parker Road
Baltimore, Maryland 21227

Commercial Sources of Large-size Multicolor Printed Reproductions

Artext Prints
Westport, Connecticut 06880

Shorewood Reproductions
724 Fifth Avenue
New York, New York 10019

Harry N. Abrams, Inc.
6 West 57th Street
New York, New York 10019

Art Education
Blauvelt, New York 10913

Commercial Sources of Filmstrips for Art Educators

Alesco
404 Sette Drive
Paramus, New Jersey 08652

Coronet Instructional Media
65 E. South Water Street
Chicago, Illinois 60601

Audio Visual Division
Educational Reading Services
320 Route 17
Mahwah, New Jersey 07430

Educational Unlimited Corporation
Media Unlimited Division
13001 Puritan Avenue
Detroit, Michigan 48227

Encyclopedia Britannica Educational Corp.
425 North Michigan Avenue
Chicago, Illinois 60611

Singer Society for Visual Education, Inc.
1345 Diversey Parkway
Chicago, Illinois 60614

Argus Communications
3505 North Ashland Avenue
Chicago, Illinois 60657

Association Instructional Materials
866 Third Avenue
New York, New York 10022

BFA Educational Media
Division of Columbia Broadcasting System, Inc.
2211 Michigan Avenue
Santa Monica, California 90404

Educational Dimensions Corporation
25–60 Francis Lewis Boulevard
Flushing, New York 11358

Rand McNally and Company
Box 7600
Chicago, Illinois 60680

Universal Education and Visual Arts
221 Park Avenue South
Dept. F.S-1
New York, New York 10003

Visuals for Teaching
P.O. Box 8455
Universal City, California 91608

Warren Schloat Productions, Inc.
Pleasantville, New York 10570

Eye Gate
146-01 Archer Avenue
Jamaica, New York 11435

Material Available Free from the National Gallery of Art

Each of the following slide lectures consists of 40 or more 35-mm color slides or film strip, a phonograph recording, and a copy of the disc text in printed form. The slides can be used in any standard air-cooled projector and may be kept for two weeks. The filmstrip sets each consist of a 35-mm single-frame filmstrip and an accompanying

188

printed text. The filmstrips can be shown in any standard filmstrip projector and, like the slide sets, may be kept for two weeks.

Please be sure to give *at least* one month advance notice. Write to: Extension Services, National Gallery of Art, Washington, D.C. 20565.

a. Slide lectures.

700 Years of Art. The great epochs of art are vividly contrasted to show how cultural ideals, social customs, and art itself have developed in Western countries from 1200 to the present day. 60 slides.

Survey of American Painting. This lecture shows the development of American painting from the "primitives" of our new young country to the modern movements of the twentieth century. Works by Copley, West, Stuart, Inness, Homer, Eakins, Ryder, Henri, Bellows, Marin, and many others are discussed. 40 slides.

Backgrounds of Modern Painting in France. The colorful works of the Impressionists and Post-Impressionists are featured as they developed out of the academic and realistic trends of the last century. 40 slides.

Five Techniques of Painting. The secret of the old masters' colors are explored and their methods of working reconstructed. 40 slides.

American Textiles. Watercolor renderings from the Index of American Design illustrate various fabric weaves, patterns, and needlework in examples of textiles used most frequently in America between 1700 and 1900. 60 slides.

Introduction to Understanding Art. A selection of the Gallery's paintings, sculptures, ceramics, and tapestries is used to establish fundamental artistic aims in various arts at different periods. A useful introduction to art appreciation is presented in simple terms. 40 slides.

The Christmas Story in Art. The story of Christ's infancy, from the Annunciation to the Flight into Egypt, illustrated in paintings. 40 slides.

The Easter Story in Art. Episodes from the entry into Jerusalem on Palm Sunday through Christ's passion and ascension are illustrated by paintings and prints from the National Gallery's collections. 50 slides.

Paintings of the Great Spanish Masters. This lecture includes the major painters of Spain from those who worked at the court of Ferdinand and Isabella to Picasso and Dali. 50 slides.

Famous Men and Women in Portraits. The lecture briefly traces the development of portraiture in Western art and then considers well-known figures of history as artists have represented them. 50 slides.

Color and Light in Painting. This lecture illustrates relationships between light and color, and shows how painters have made use of color. 50 slides.

Line, Plane, and Form in Pictorial Composition. Important changes in pictorial composition are traced through the styles of Byzantium, the Gothic period, the Renaissance, Mannerism, Baroque, and Rococo to more recent developments, including Cubism. 50 slides.

Physics and Painting. The changes in thought about the structure of the physical world are reflected in artistic changes from the Middle Ages to the present. 32 slides.

The Creative Past: Art of Africa.

b. Color filmstrip sets.

American Painting in History. This lecture illustrates the relationship between American painting and the growth and development of our country with a selection of pictures from the "primitives" to the twentieth-century artists of America. Views of historic buildings and other objects are included. Presentation is adapted to the elementary school and is organized in six one-minute lectures. 60 pictures.

Florentine Art of the Golden Age. The development of Florentine painting and sculpture in the fifteenth century is illustrated with the history of the city and certain of its famous personages and buildings. Suitable material for both art and history classes, adaptable to elementary or advanced schools. A short bibliography is included. 56 pictures.

c. 16-mm sound-color films.

The following 16-mm color sound motion pictures may be borrowed at no cost for a three-day period. The borrower pays return postage and postal insurance for the value listed with each film. The borrower is responsible for any damage or loss while the film is in his possession. To avoid damage, an experienced projectionist and up-to-date projector are recommended. Please order at least three months before requested showing date and provide alternate dates and titles.

To book films write to: Extension Services, National Gallery of Art, Washington, D.C. 20565.

To Know How to See. The background and creative work of Leonardo da Vinci. 60 minutes.

American Vision. Pictures from the National Gallery of Art trace the development of American painting from pre-revolutionary days to the beginning of the twentieth century. 35 minutes.

In Search of Rembrandt. A National Gallery of Art

Documentary film portrait of Rembrandt as seen through his work. 50 minutes.

Time Enough to See a World. Paintings from the Rennaissance to the twentieth century are analyzed for their composition and for the way they reflect their cultural background. 30 minutes.

Art in the Western World. This film describes the National Gallery of Art from its inception and focuses on the most outstanding paintings and sculpture in its collections. 30 minutes.

The National Gallery of Art. This film highlights the Gallery's collection and its varied audience. 50 minutes.

A Gallery of Children. Mrs. Joan Kennedy takes a group of children on a tour of the National Gallery of Art, meeting children in paintings from many ages of history. Elementary level. 30 minutes.

Index